Oxford New Geography 4
a course for juniors
Keith Martin
Series Editor: Gordon Elliott

Contents

Oxford University Press

Looking at buildings

We often take buildings for granted. We know they are there but we don't look very closely at them. In this unit we are going to find out how to look at buildings.

A memory test

Think of your school.
What is the roof made of?
What are the walls built of?
What colour is the front door?
What date was the school built?
How do you know? Whose room is nearest to the front door? Check your answers when you next go around the school.

Postcard quiz

Here are some postcards of famous buildings. Where are they? The labels have been mixed up. Copy out the names of the buildings and put the correct country next to each one.

1   Eiffel Tower — Australia
2   Pyramids — India
3   Buckingham Palace — Egypt
4   Sydney Opera House — England
5   Taj Mahal — France

Contrasts

Many buildings are places for people to live in. On the facing page are pictures and plans of two houses: a country mansion and a shanty dwelling.

Perhaps you have visited a country mansion. Many are now open for the public to look around. A small part, where the owners live, is left private. Shanty dwellings are homes for many poor people living on the edge of cities, for example, in South America, Africa and South East Asia.

The two buildings are very different. Look carefully at them both. Would you prefer to live in a mansion or a shanty? Write down reasons for your answer.

Country mansion

Shanty

This would be the size of the shanty if it was drawn to the same scale as the mansion.

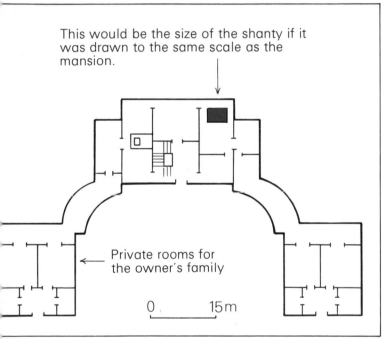

← Private rooms for the owner's family

0   15 m

Plan of mansion

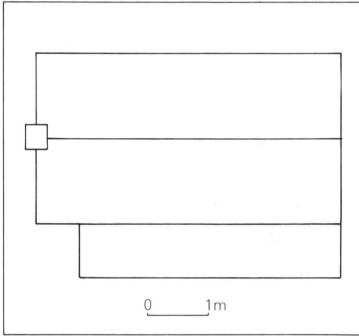

0   1 m

Plan of shanty

Compare the two buildings by copying out this chart and filling in the spaces. In the final column, fill in the details for your own house.

	Mansion	Shanty	My house
How big is the house?			
What are the walls built of?			
What is the roof made of?			
How many rooms are there?			
How many windows are there?			

Close-up on buildings

You can use the information on these two pages to help you take a closer look at buildings around you.

Types of house

Bungalow

Detached house

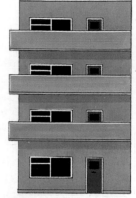
Flat

Terraced house

Semi-detached house

Windows

Sash window — opens upwards and downwards

Casement window — opens outwards

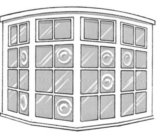
Bay window with 'bull's eye' pane of glass

Pivoted window with metal frame

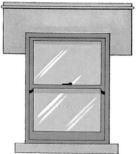
Dripstone course round the top of window to stop rainwater running down

Doors

Wooden panelled door

Door with glass panel

Doorway with porch — the supporting columns can be made of wood or stone

Door with fanlight above to give more light inside

Footscraper at doorway — what would it be used for? What does this tell you about the original state of the road?

4

Plaques, dates and signs

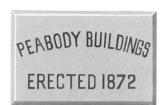

Datestone

PEABODY BUILDINGS
ERECTED 1872

Benefactor's or builder's plaque (sometimes initials only) to show who had the house built

EDGAR WALLACE 1875–1932 Writer lived here

Plaque to show that the house was the birthplace of an important person

JUBILEE TERRACE

Commemorative sign – this terrace was built at the time of Queen Victoria's Jubilee.

House styles

Can you find any houses like these near you? Beware of imitations: some styles have been copied at later times. Some houses have a mixture of styles.

Tudor – wooden framed house with black painted beams

Georgian – elegant terrace

Victorian – terraced houses

1930s semi-detached house

New housing estate

What is a house made of?

Roof

Slate

Tile

Decorated tile

Thatch

Walls

Brick

Stone

Timber

Concrete blocks

Brickwork patterns

English bond

Flemish bond

Stretcher bond

Corner decorations

Look closely at the houses you pass on the way to school. Write some sentences about the information you can find out by looking at houses.

For example, count how many chimneys there are on a house. What could this tell you about the number of heated rooms? If there are no chimney pots, how might the house be heated?

5

Spring Street Survey

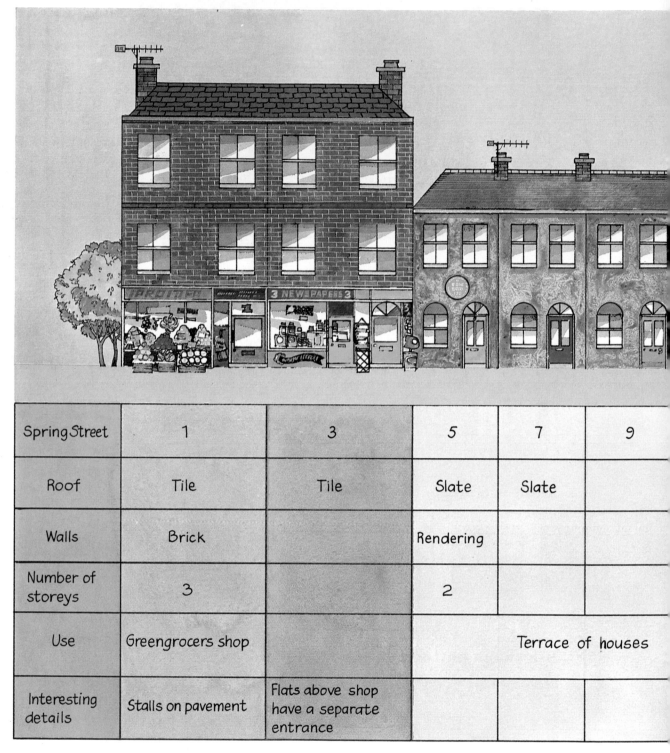

Spring Street	1	3	5	7	9
Roof	Tile	Tile	Slate	Slate	
Walls	Brick		Rendering		
Number of storeys	3		2		
Use	Greengrocers shop			Terrace of houses	
Interesting details	Stalls on pavement	Flats above shop have a separate entrance			

This is Spring Street. Class 4 went out with their teacher and took a close look at the buildings.

What number in Spring Street is the newsagent's? Which is the oldest building in the street? Which is the newest? Which buildings would be empty during the night?

Below the picture is a chart which class 4 made so that they could record what they saw in the street. Some of the information still has to be filled in. Copy out the chart and complete the survey of Spring Street.

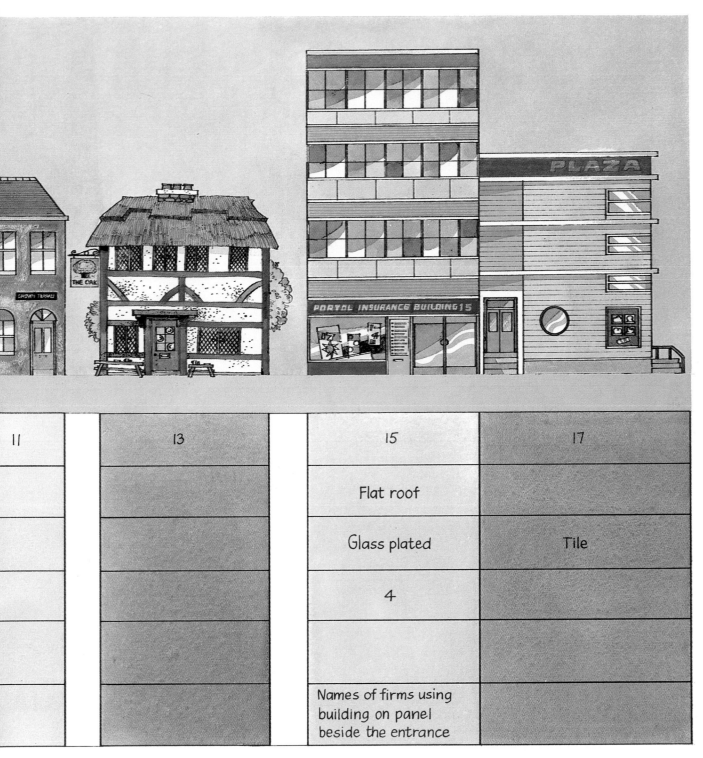

11	13	15	17
		Flat roof	
		Glass plated	Tile
		4	
		Names of firms using building on panel beside the entrance	

The buildings in Spring Street are not all the same shape or size. This could make the street look interesting. It might make some buildings look out of place. Which do you think is true for Spring Street?

Make a survey of a street near your school. Draw a chart and put in the five headings. Use the information shown on pages 5 and 6 to help you.

7

Checking

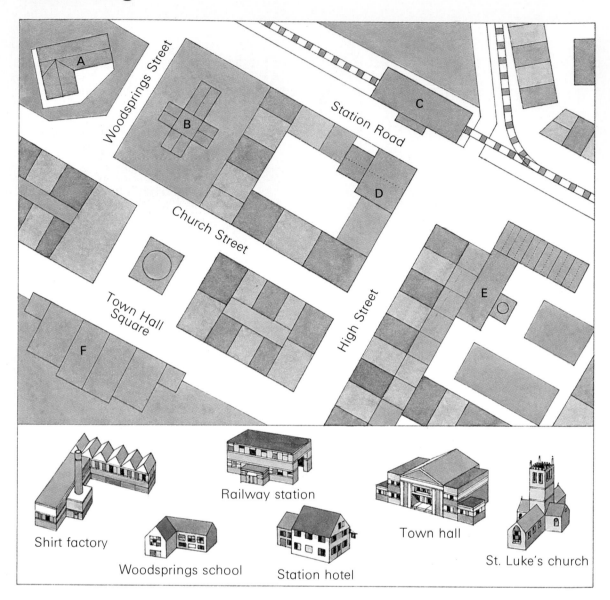

Shirt factory

Railway station

Woodsprings school

Station hotel

Town hall

St. Luke's church

Thinking

1 This street plan shows many buildings. There are pictures of some of the buildings below the plan.

Find the buildings on the plan. Each building is shown by a letter. Write down the names of each building, followed by the correct letter. Look carefully at the shape of each building to help you decide its correct place on the plan.

2 Describe two routes from Woodsprings school to the shirt factory. What would you see on the way?

Doing

1 Make a list of the most important buildings in your town. What are they used for?

2 Describe and draw
(a) your favourite building;
(b) the ugliest building you have ever seen.

3 Draw your house: the front view and a plan. Mark all the interesting details.

Puzzle corner

Look at the pictures of a city. Can you name it? Collect pictures of buildings from a different city. Cut out the pictures and make a collage of the city. Can your neighbour name it?

Going further

When people buy a house they often ask for details of houses for sale from an estate agent. Here are the details of Cosy Nook.

ESTATE AGENTS

FOR SALE : COSY NOOK

A delightful old cottage in the sleepy village of Little Bindweed, five miles from the nearest town. The property is built of stone with a thatched roof. It is in good decorative order and enjoys fine views over open countryside.

The accomodation comprises:

ENTRANCE HALL   Built-in cupboard.
Door to:

LOUNGE   12' x 12'; attractive bay window at rear, large fireplace, ceiling with oak beams, two electric points.

KITCHEN   10' x 8'; sink unit, cupboards, three electric points.

A staircase from the lounge leads to:

THE FIRST FLOOR

BEDROOM   11' x 10'; built-in wardrobe.

BATHROOM   Panelled bath, pedestal wash basin, WC.

OUTSIDE

Large garden: lawn and flower beds at front of cottage, kitchen garden and orchard at rear.

RATES............ £250 a year.

OFFERS IN THE REGION OF £30,000

1   What is Cosy Nook built of? What is the roof made of? How many rooms are there upstairs? How many rooms are there downstairs? Would a family with three children buy Cosy Nook? Would the house be suitable for a retired couple who liked gardening? Would you like to live in Cosy Nook? Give reasons for your answers.

2   Write an estate agent's description of your own house.

3   Imagine your school is going to be sold. Write the estate agent's details which would make people want to buy the school.

9

Our town then and now

Most people live in or near towns but they don't often explore them. Exploring towns can be exciting and interesting because they are always changing. By looking closely at a town, you can find evidence of its past. You can also trace changes up to the present day.

The town you are looking at in this unit is Wareham, a small town in Dorset. Find Wareham in an atlas.

Old photographs can show how a town has changed through the years. This is an old photograph of Wareham. It was taken at the crossroads in the centre of the

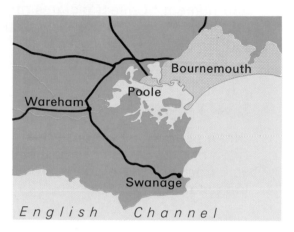

town. People are standing in the street chatting to one another. Would they be able to stand in the middle of the street today? Why not?

Here is a close-up picture of the street lamp in the photograph. What kind of lamp is it? What do you think the two bars sticking out below the glass lantern are used for? How are street lamps lit today?

Here is the same view of Wareham today. Look carefully at the two photographs and identify the same buildings in each one. Find the Red Lion Inn.

Make a list of the differences between the two photographs. Use these headings to help you: **vehicles, buildings, road signs, people's clothes, street lamps**. Spot any other differences which are not covered by these headings.

Which picture has this shape in it? What is it?

Which words from the following list would you choose to describe each picture: quiet, busy, peaceful, noisy, dangerous, pleasant, attractive, cluttered, calm, littered, ugly, clean? Write a description of each picture using the words you have chosen.

Puzzle corner

This is the gateway to the Red Lion Inn. Why is it so large?
Clue — inside is a courtyard, a horse trough and the remains of some stables.

Looking at old maps

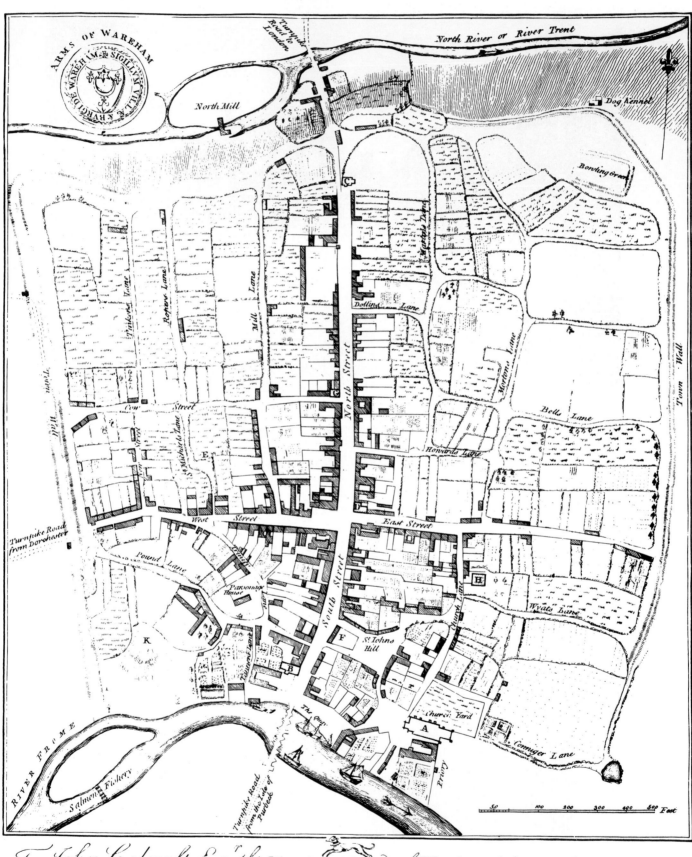

ARMS OF WAREHAM · SIGILLVM VILLE · BVRGI DE WAREHAM

Turnpike Road to London

North River or River Trent

Dog Kennel

North Mill

Bondingören

Trükets Lane

Ropere Lane

Mill Lane

North Street

Dollins Lane

Mortons Lane

Town Wall

Cow Street

St Michaels Lane

E

Howards Lane

Bells Lane

Turnpike Road from Dorchester

West Street

East Street

Pound Lane

South Street

Church Lane

H

Wyats Lane

Parsonage House

F St Johns Hill

K

B

Church Yard

A

RIVER FROME

The Quay

Cornishgt Lane

Salmon Fishery

Turnpike Road from the Isle of Purbeck

Priory

50 100 200 300 400 500 Feet

To John Calcraft Esq.ʳ this Plan of Wareham, is humbly inscribed by The Author.

A. St Mary's Church.
B. Trinity Church.
C. St Martin's Church.
D. Town Hall formerly St Peter's Church.
E. Formerly St Michael's Church.
F. Formerly St John's Church.
G. Formerly Allhallon's Chapel.
H. Dissenter's Meeting House.
I. Alms House.
K. Formerly the Castle.

This is a map of Wareham in 1774. It shows the town buildings, the streets and the fields belonging to the townspeople. The town is enclosed on three sides by the town wall. It was built to defend the town from invaders. What protected the fourth side of the town? Follow the outline of the wall with your finger.

This is the town wall today. Only the earth bank remains. The picture was taken where Cow Street meets the town wall. Find it on the map.

This section is known as Bloody Bank because executions used to take place here. After the executions the heads of the victims were displayed on pikestaffs on South Bridge by the quay.

Two street signs as they are today

Find these places on the map:

Quay — Wareham was once an important port. Cargoes of grain, salt and potter's clay were shipped to France from here.

Bowling green — This is the site of an Elizabethan bowling green. Town fairs were also held here.

Mill Lane — The lane leads to North Mill on the River Trent.

Castle Mound (K) — This is the site of a Norman castle.

St. Martin's Church (C) — This is the oldest church in Dorset. It was built in 1020.

St. Mary's Church (A) — The church contains the coffin of Edward the Martyr who was stabbed by his stepmother at nearby Corfe Castle. His bones were removed and buried in Shaftesbury.

Crossroads — The four main streets of the town extend from the crossroads in the centre like the points of a compass. Look at the names of the streets. Most of the houses are along these four main streets.

Study the map carefully and answer the questions.

1   Look at the shape of the crossroads area. Where were the photographs on pages 10 and 11 taken?
2   How would you describe the shape of Wareham?
3   There are three main routes into Wareham. Where do they come from?
4   Find these lanes on the map: Ropers Lane, Tinkers Lane, Pound Lane, Tanners Lane. Their names tell you something about the activities that were carried on there. Match the correct lane to each of the following: leather-working, rope-making, selling pots and pans, rounding up stray animals.

Making a trail

One way of exploring a town is to make a town trail. Plan a route through the town. Choose stopping points. These could include:

Important places — town hall, river bridge

Historical places — market cross, church, castle

Interesting places — quayside, an old street

Busy places — market, shopping centre, main street

Quiet places — park, river-side

Ugly places — littered street, shack, factory

Changing places — building site, new road scheme

Make a list of things to do at each stopping place. For example, look, listen, smell, draw, take photographs and tape-record sounds.

Class 4 made a town trail of Wareham. Here are some of the things they noted.

Things from the past

This is the quay. It is no longer used as a port for goods but as a mooring place for pleasure boats. Some children are drawing the scene. They are noting the names of the boats and where they come from. Some are finding out what the old granary on the quayside was used for in the past and what it is used for now.

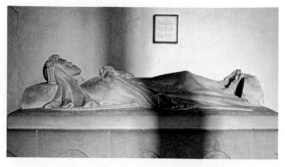

This is the inside of St. Martin's Church. The statue is of Lawrence of Arabia, a hero of the First World War, who lived near Wareham.

Contrasts

Ladies Walk and North Street are within ten metres of each other.

Lucy drew this picture of Ladies Walk. It is a quiet and peaceful place. You can hear birds singing. It was named after the ladies who paraded their fine Sunday clothes on their way home from church.

Mark took this photograph of North Street. It is a noisy, bustling place with a lot of traffic.

This sign can be seen on some of the houses in Wareham. It is the mark of Rempstone Estate. All houses owned by the estate bore this sign.

Sounds and smells

This is the market. Market day is an important day in Wareham. Cattle can no longer be bought but fresh vegetables and other items are sold on the stalls or auctioned in the market hall.

This unusual inn sign is in South Street.

This sign is for the Anglebury Cafe. It shows the town's coat of arms.

Signs

This is a fire mark. Houses bearing this sign were insured against fire. The fire brigades were owned by insurance companies and would only put out a fire if a house had this sign.

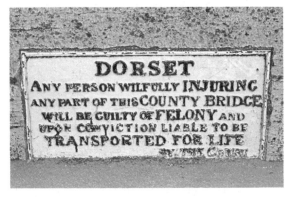

This sign on North Bridge is to stop vandalism. Where would offenders have been transported to?

Checking

Thinking

This is a map of Wareham today.

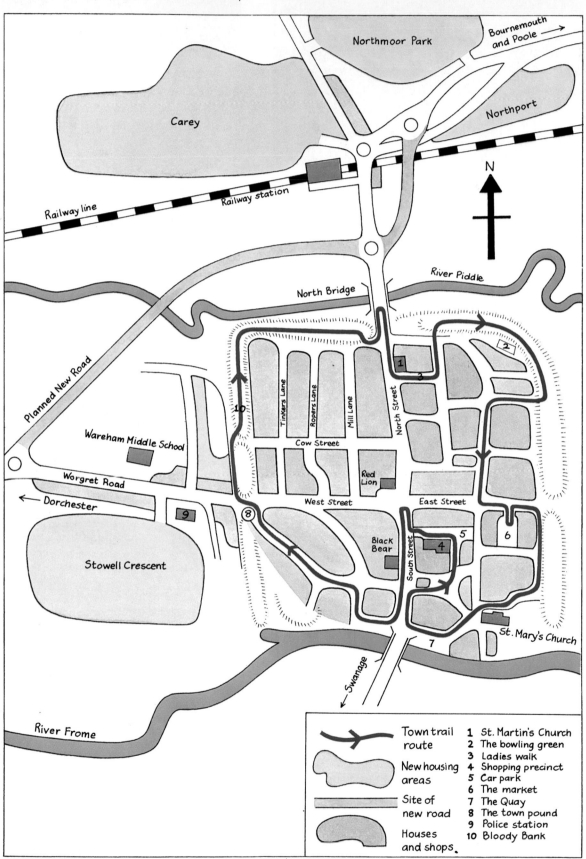

Northmoor Park

Bournemouth and Poole →

Carey

Northport

Railway line

Railway station

N

River Piddle

North Bridge

Planned New Road

Tinkers Lane

Ropers Lane

Mill Lane

Cow Street

North Street

1

2

3

Wareham Middle School

10

Worgret Road

Red Lion

West Street

East Street

← Dorchester

9

8

5

6

Black Bear

South Street

4

Stowell Crescent

7

St. Mary's Church

Swanage →

River Frome

↦ Town trail route	1	St. Martin's Church
	2	The bowling green
New housing areas	3	Ladies walk
	4	Shopping precinct
Site of new road	5	Car park
	6	The market
	7	The Quay
Houses and shops.	8	The town pound
	9	Police station
	10	Bloody Bank

16

1 The town trail route is marked on this map. Follow the trail and find these places: Bloody Bank, the town wall, North Bridge, St. Martin's Church, Ladies Walk, the bowling green, the market, St. Mary's Church, the quay, the crossroads, the Red Lion Inn and the town pound. Look back over the unit and write a sentence about each one.

2 Why are there no houses between the railway station and the old town? **Clue** — the land by the river is very low-lying.

3 This map of Wareham shows a much larger area than the old map on page 12. Look at the old map and find out where it would fit on the map of Wareham today. Is the street pattern still the same? Name three things on today's map that were not there in 1774.

Going further

1 How do towns get their names? Wareham gets its name from the weir on the river. 'Ham' means 'home' so that Wareham is 'home by the weir'. Here are some more town endings and their meanings.

ley — by a river (Chor**ley**)
tun, ton — village (Bol**ton**)
stead — enclosed place (Hamp**stead**)
worth — estate (Chats**worth**)
staple — store (Barn**staple**)
chester — roman camp (Man**chester**)
caster — roman camp (Don**caster**)
cester — roman camp (Wor**cester**)
shot — wood (Alder**shot**)
by — settlement (Whit**by**)
thwaite — farm (Husthwaite)
thorpe — village (Mable**thorpe**)
wich — settlement (Nor**wich**)

How did your town get its name? Find out the meanings of the names of other towns in your area.

2 Use a tape-recorder to make a sound trail of your town. Think of the different sounds that would make a sound picture. They might include some of the following: a clock chiming, the bustle of a market, factory noises, traffic, trains, a paper seller's cry, a football crowd, lapping water.

After taping the sounds, play them back to your class. Can they guess what the sounds are and where they were recorded? You could take photographs of the places and show them while playing the sounds.

3 Here are some objects collected by children from Wareham as part of an exhibition called **Our town then and now**. Make a similar exhibition for your town.

Looking at open spaces

Here is a picture of a park in a town. The park has been provided to give people who live in the town an area of open space away from all the buildings. Look at all the things which are happening in the picture. Make a list of the activities you can see under these headings: **sport, games for children, places to walk, colourful areas, open areas.** Which of the activities could you find in your own local park?

In large cities many people may live a long distance from any open space. Sometimes empty building sites are turned into adventure playgrounds for children. If there are no parks or adventure playgrounds nearby where would city children play?

Look at the two pictures on this page. Which area would you like to play in? Why? Where do you play?

Beyond the towns and cities is the countryside. Much of it is farmland but there are large areas where people can enjoy the fresh air, appreciate the scenery and get away from the crowds. Look at the picture and list the activities showing people enjoying the countryside. Two of the people in the picture are working. Who are they? What are they doing?

Boundaries in the countryside

Here are some of the boundaries used to divide up farming land and separate it from open spaces where people can walk.

Hedges You can get a rough idea of the age of a hedge by counting the number of different kinds of plants in 30 metres of hedge. Multiply this number by 100 and you have the approximate age of the hedge in years.

Fences Electric fences are used to stop cattle straying.

Stone walls In some parts of England there are many miles of dry stone walling. The stones are very carefully laid so that they do not need mortar to keep them in place.

Can you think of any other ways of dividing up the countryside?

National Parks in Britain

Large areas of the most beautiful countryside in Britain have been made into National Parks. This has been done to stop the areas being spoilt. Towns and industry are not allowed to spread into the parks. Instead they remain as large open spaces of countryside where people can go to look at the scenery and enjoy many outdoor activities.

The pictures on this page show some of the things which people can do in the parks. Match each of these activities to the correct picture: walking, climbing, fishing, pony-trekking, sailing, pot-holing, camping.

Look at the pictures. Choose which activities you would like to do.

1 Northumberland
2 Lake District
5 Peak District
8 Brecon Beacons
10 Dartmoor

This map shows the ten National Parks in Britain. Some of them are named in the key. Use an atlas to find the names of the other parks.

The map also shows the parts of Britain where there are large towns and cities clustered together. These groups of towns are called conurbations. Some are named on the map. Use an atlas to find the names of the other conurbations.

Which National Parks are nearest to Manchester, Newcastle, Bristol, Birmingham, your home? Which National Park is furthest away from a conurbation? Which park is likely to have the most visitors?

By using motorways people from the cities can reach the National Parks easily and quickly. During summer weekends the roads in the parks are very busy. They are full of cars and the small villages become choked with people.

Look at the picture below. It was taken at Ambleside in the Lake District National Park on a Sunday afternoon. Compare it with one of the pictures on the opposite page. What differences do you notice? Which picture do you prefer? Where might the people have come from? What would the street look like on a Monday morning?

A walk in the country

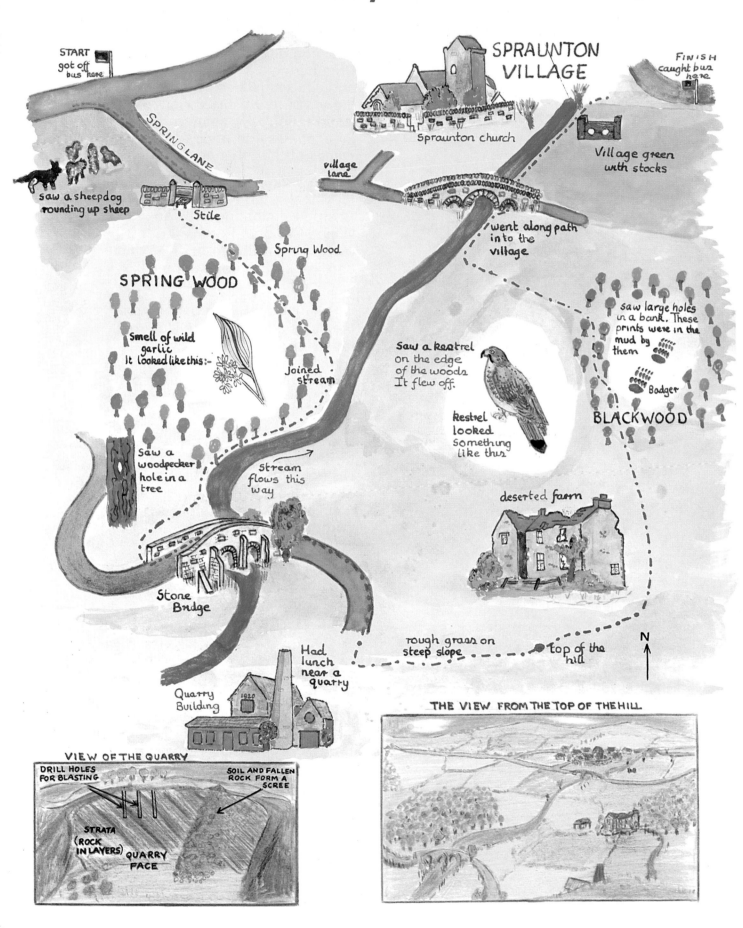

START got off bus here

SPRING LANE

saw a sheepdog rounding up sheep

Stile

SPRAUNTON VILLAGE

Spraunton church

FINISH caught bus here

Village green with stocks

village lane

went along path into the village

SPRING WOOD

Spring Wood

Smell of wild garlic It looked like this:-

Joined stream

Saw a kestrel on the edge of the woods It flew off.

kestrel looked something like this

saw large holes in a bank. These prints were in the mud by them

Badger

BLACKWOOD

Saw a woodpecker hole in a tree

Stream flows this way

deserted farm

Stone Bridge

Had lunch near a quarry

Quarry Building 1920

rough grass on steep slope

top of the hill

N

VIEW OF THE QUARRY

DRILL HOLES FOR BLASTING

SOIL AND FALLEN ROCK FORM A SCREE

STRATA (ROCK IN LAYERS) QUARRY FACE

THE VIEW FROM THE TOP OF THE HILL

David has drawn a map of a country walk. Follow his route and look at the things he noticed on his walk. Look carefully at David's map and answer these questions.

1 Where did David see the woodpecker holes?
2 Where did he see the badger footprints?
3 Where did he see the stocks?
4 Where did he see the kestrel?
5 Where did he have his lunch?
6 What did David call 'strata'?
7 What did he mean by the word 'scree'?
8 How did he know that the rock had been blasted from the face of the quarry?

David took a compass with him on his walk so that he could tell in which direction he was walking. Here is David's compass.

Whichever way you turn the compass case, the needle always points to north. Around the edge of the compass are the initials of the main directions. These are called compass points. **N** stands for north. **E** stands for east. **SW** stands for south west. Write out in full the names of all the compass points.

Two things for you to do

1 Tell the story of David's walk in your own words.
2 Go on an exploration walk of your own. Make a picture map of the route to include things of interest that you see on the way.

How to use a compass

1 Face the direction in which you wish to go.

2 Hold the compass flat and turn it until the needle is pointing to the **N** marked on the rim.

3 Read the compass point for the direction you are facing. By keeping a check on the compass you can see if you are travelling in the direction you want to go.

David has put a direction pointer on his map to show which way is north. In which direction was he travelling (a) when he made his climb up to the top of the hill; (b) when he walked upstream through the wood?

At the top of the hill where he drew the picture of the view, David made this direction chart. Copy it out and put in the compass direction for each arrow.

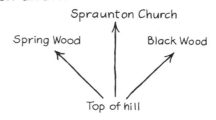

Spraunton Church

Spring Wood   Black Wood

Top of hill

Checking

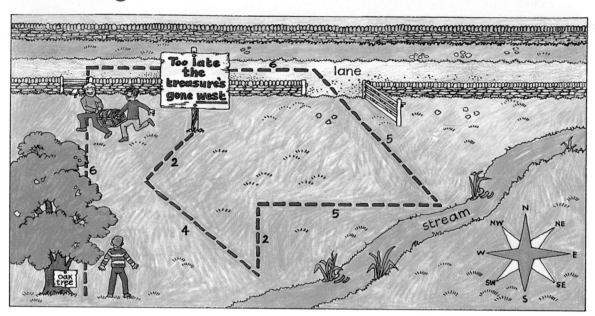

Follow the trail

David and his friends made up a treasure trail using compass directions. Read the instructions and follow the trail on the picture.

Start at the oak tree. Go 6 paces N. Turn E. Walk forward 6 paces along the lane. Walk 5 paces in a SE direction to the stream. Turn W and walk 5 paces. Go S for 2 paces. Don't fall in the stream! Walk 4 paces NW and then 2 paces NE. Here lies the treasure.

David was too late. See if you are more successful with the treasure trail below. Trace the picture. Be careful to mark everything in its correct position. Follow the instructions and find out where the treasure is hidden. Measure 1 centimetre to represent 1 pace.

Start at X. Go 4 paces E; 5 paces NE; 2 paces N; 7 paces W; 3 paces SW and 1 pace S. Here lies the treasure. You will need a bucket and some rope.

Doing

1   Use a compass to make your own treasure trail. Draw a map of it and write out the instructions. Try it on your friends. Can they follow the course?

2   Make a collection of pictures and maps from different National Parks in Britain. Draw a large map of Britain showing the parks. Arrange the pictures around the map, linking them to the correct park.

3   There are also National Parks in other countries in the world. Here are pictures of three of them. Find out where they are.

Yellowstone National Park

Etosha National Park

Going further

1   Design an adventure playground for children. You can get some ideas from the one on page 18. You could include things to climb, to crawl through and to swing on.

2   Make a list of open spaces near your home. Put them under these headings: **countryside, parks and recreation grounds, waste ground.**

3   Could you improve an open space near your home? Draw plans to show how you could make a site in your town more attractive.

4   Learn the **Country Code:**

Guard against all risk of fire.

Fasten all gates.

Keep dogs under proper control.

Keep to paths across farm land.

Avoid damaging fences, hedges and walls.

Leave no litter.

Safeguard water supplies.

Protect wild life, wild plants and trees.

Go carefully on country roads.

Respect the life of the countryside.

Manyara National Park

Exploring the weather

Out in the Atlantic Ocean a storm is raging. On board the weather ship **Explorer** the radio officer is sending details of the storm to the meteorological office in Britain.

Date: 20th Jan 1980
Time: 12 noon
Wind: South West
Storm Force 10
Sky: Overcast
Heavy showers of rain
Visibility: Poor
Sea: Very rough

The meteorological office receives reports from weather ships and weather stations all over the country. The reports are studied and put together to build up a complete picture of the weather.

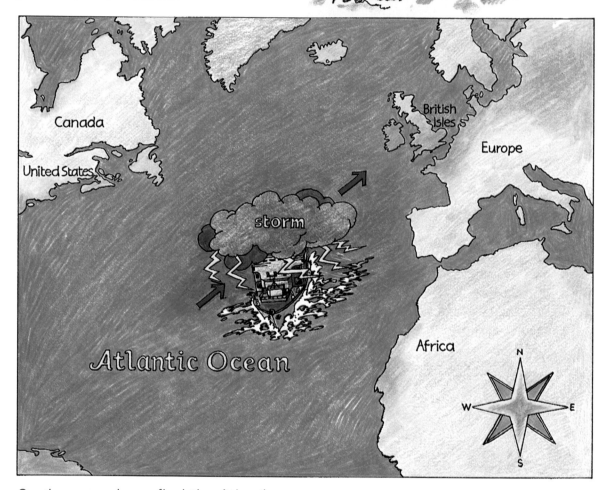

On the map above find the Atlantic Ocean, the weather ship **Explorer** and the storm. The arrows show the direction of the wind. Check the radio officer's message about the wind. Is it correct? Which country is in the path of the storm?

This is the radio officer's log where he keeps a record of his messages. Copy it out and fill in the entries he would make.

Weather ship Explorer
Date _____
Time _____
Wind direction _____
Wind strength _____
Cloud cover _____
Rainfall _____
Visibility _____
State of sea _____

When the meteorological office received the report from the **Explorer** they broadcast this gale warning on the radio.

Here is a gale warning for midnight 20th January 1980. Severe gale imminent for sea areas Sole, Plymouth, Shannon and Fastnet.

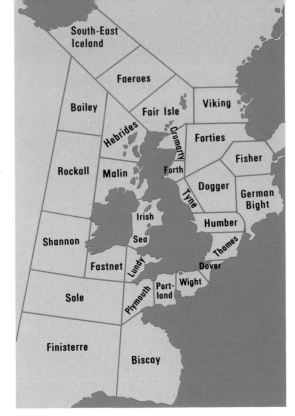

These people were listening to the broadcast. Why would they be anxious to know if a gale was approaching?

The gale warning mentions four sea areas. Find them on the map. Why will the gale reach Sole before Humber?

You remember that wind speed is measured with an anemometer. It is graded by giving it a number from 0 to 12 on the Beaufort Scale. Below is a chart of the 12 strengths.

0. Calm
1. Light Air
2. Light Breeze
3. Gentle Breeze
4. Moderate Breeze
5. Fresh Breeze
6. Strong Breeze
7. Near Gale
8. Gale
9. Strong Gale
10. Storm
11. Violent Storm
12. Hurricane

Storm damage

Gales and storm winds can do great damage. They cause huge waves at sea which break with tremendous force when they reach the coast.

The picture shows storm waves breaking over the coastal town of Torcross in January 1979. Many of the buildings along the sea front were badly damaged by the force of the waves. Some collapsed into the sea. Huge boulders were picked up by the waves and tossed on to the buildings causing further damage. The sea also flooded low-lying areas inland.

Here are some words that describe the wind and sea in a storm. Copy out the list and fill in the missing letters.

Gale force winds
b - ow - ng
gu - ti - g
wh - s - lin -
- oar - - g
h - - l - ng

Towering waves
r - llin -
swe - l - - g
b - ea - - ng
s - ash- n -
cr - s - i - -

Use the words to help you write a poem describing a storm at sea or on the coast.

The pictures below show the collapse of the Tacoma Bridge in the USA in 1940. The collapse was caused by the force of the wind. The wind started the suspension bridge swinging and created a wave pattern along it until the roadway broke up and the bridge fell into the river below. Describe what is happening in each of the four pictures. Imagine you were driving the last car to cross the bridge. Tell the story.

Strong winds while snow is falling can create blizzards. These are heavy snowfalls which are driven at high speed by the wind. Large drifts are quickly formed and it becomes difficult to see very far.

The picture shows a blizzard in the Cairngorms, a range of mountains in Scotland. The walkers are struggling against the wind. At times like this it can be very dangerous in the mountains. People become tired quickly in these conditions. They get very cold and begin to suffer from exposure.

Safety in the mountains

The pictures tell the story of two groups of walkers on a mountain hike. Kate and her friends behave sensibly, Phil and his friends do not.

Look at each set of pictures and write some sentences to say what lessons Phil and his friends could learn from Kate and her friends.

1. Careful Kate takes the right things needed on a hike.
2. She informs someone of route and time back.
3. Kate and her friends take shelter during blizzard.

1. Foolish Phil
2.
3.

The weather forecast

This is Michael Fish, one of the television weathermen, giving a forecast of the weather for the British Isles. The symbols on the map are a quick way of showing the type of weather in different parts of the country. What kind of weather is being forecast for the following places: London, the north of Scotland, Wales, your own area?

Watch the weather forecast on television. Copy this chart and fill in the spaces in the first column with details of the forecast for your area. The following day, complete the second column and see how correct the forecast was.

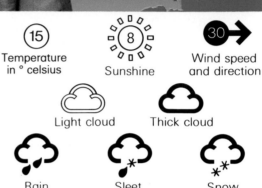

	Television forecast	What the weather was like
Temperature		
Wind		
Sun		
Cloud		
Rain		
Snow		
Sleet		

Weather forecasters gather information from many sources. Some are shown on the opposite page. What are they? By looking at all the information, the weather forecasters are then able to make a forecast about the weather for the following day.

Look at the maps below. Can you make a weather forecast for 6 p.m. on Thursday?

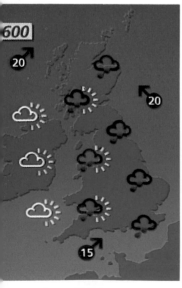

6 am Wednesday

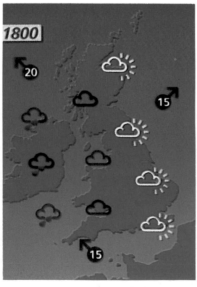

6 pm Wednesday

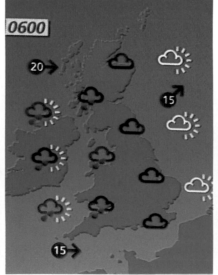

6 am Thursday

6 pm Thursday

Where the information comes from

Weather balloons Instruments in the box below the balloon measure and record conditions high above the earth's surface.

Weather ships The ships send detailed reports of weather conditions out at sea.

Land weather stations Records of the weather are kept and daily reports made.

Weather satellites These are orbiting round the earth. Cameras on board the satellite take photographs which show the weather patterns and cloud formations. The photographs are sent back to earth as radio signals. The signals are then converted back to photographs and used for weather forecasting. Satellite weather photographs are often shown on the TV weather forecast.

Here is a weather photograph taken from a satellite. It shows the North Atlantic Ocean. Find the British Isles. The white areas are clouds. A large spiral of cloud is approaching the British Isles from the west. The outer edge of the cloud spiral is already covering parts of the country. Look closely at the photograph. Copy the chart and tick the correct box to show the cloud cover in each area.

Area	Clear Sky	Cloudy
Scotland		
Ireland		
Wales		
Northern England		
South West England		
France		

By looking at the photograph, weather men are able to forecast which way the clouds will move. Can you make a forecast for the British Isles?

Checking

Thinking

1 Here are pictures of some of the instruments used to observe and measure the weather. Match each name to the correct picture and say what each instrument measures.

Anemometer   Rain gauge
Thermometer   Wind vane

2 Shipping forecasts are broadcast every day. They give details of the weather in each sea area. You can hear them if you listen to BBC Radio 4 at 1.55 p.m. or 5.50 p.m. Listen to one of the forecasts. Make a note of the weather forecast for the sea area nearest you.

3 The names of these sea areas have been mixed up. Use the map on page 27 to help you sort them out. Nashnon, lanptord, gergod, bermuh, thigw, dynul.

Doing

1 Keep a record of the wind and weather for a week, using the following headings: **date**, **wind direction**, **wind strength**, **weather**. The chart at the bottom of page 27 will help you to estimate the wind strength.

Date	Wind direction	Wind strength	Weather

2 Make your own television weather map. Draw a map of the British Isles on a large piece of white card. Draw and colour the symbols shown on page 30 and cut them out. Put a blob of blu-tack on the back of each one. Now you can pretend to be Michael Fish and use the symbols to give a weather forecast for the British Isles.

Talking

1   Talk about a storm you have seen. Describe the sky, the wind, the rain, the thunder and lightning. How did you feel? Did the storm do any damage?

2   Look back at the picture of storm waves at Torcross on page 28. Discuss with a friend what is happening. What would happen when the storm was over? What could be done to prevent so much damage in the future?

Going further

1   Read the weather ship's message on page 26 and the radio broadcast on page 27. What has happened to the wind? Copy out the headings on the radio officer's log and fill in the entries for the weather today. Are there any entries you are unable to fill in?

2   Map A shows four areas from which the wind might come. Copy down the description of each area with the correct wind direction beside it — north, south, east or west.

Copy the chart and put in which wind direction will most likely bring the weather described.

Weather	Wind direction
Rain	from the
Cold weather	from the
Warm weather	from the
Dry weather	from the

3   Write out a weather forecast for the British Isles from the information shown on map B.

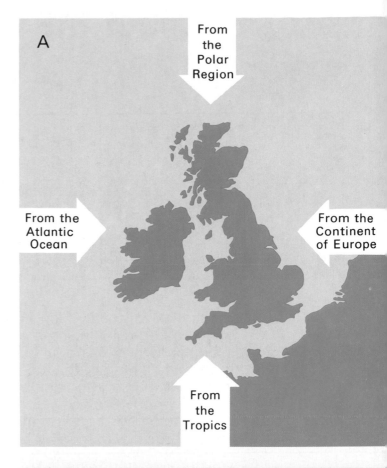

Meet the Browns of Bristol

Jeff Brown   Susan Brown   Laura Brown

. Bristol

This is the Brown family. They live in Bristol, a large city in south west England. Find Bristol in an atlas. The small map at the top of the page will help you. By looking at Bristol with the Browns you can find out what it is like to live and work in a large city.

Close your eyes and think of six things the word **city** means to you. You probably thought of some of the following: noise, bustle, crowds of people, cars, tall buildings, large shops, cinemas, offices. Write a sentence about each of the six things which mean city to you.

Working in a city centre

Jeff Brown works in a tall office block in the centre of Bristol. He says, 'I have an office on the very top floor of the block. I work for a building society which lends money to people for buying houses. I meet many people from the nearby banks during the day.

'Many firms want to have their offices in the centre of the city. This makes land very expensive to buy. There is not enough space on the ground for everyone so tall blocks are built. My office block is very new. Small houses and shops were pulled down so that the office block could be built.'

How many storeys high is the office block? How can you tell that demolition work is still going on? What can you see on the side wall of the pub? How many storeys high was the building with the fireplaces? What is the office block built of? What is the pub built of?

Why does Jeff Brown work on the top floor of his office block?
Because he asked his boss for a rise!

The Browns live near the centre of the city. They live on the tenth floor of a high-rise block of flats. They moved there when their old house was pulled down to make room for more modern buildings. From the tenth floor they have a good view of the centre of the city.

Broadmead shopping centre   Mr Brown's office   The Browns' block of flats

The photograph shows a view over the centre of Bristol. Find the Browns' block of flats and Jeff Brown's office. Follow his journey from the flat to the office. Is it short enough for him to walk? Estimate how long it would take him. The part of the journey he enjoys most is crossing the bridge over the stretch of water known as the floating harbour. There are many small boats moored there.

Look at all the office blocks. Can you see any other kinds of building? How much open space can you see in the centre of the city?

In the distance where the city sprawls out from the centre, you can see housing estates for the large number of people who work in the city. These areas are called suburbs.

35

Shopping in Bristol

Susan Brown likes to go shopping at Broadmead shopping centre. You can see the shopping centre marked on the photograph of Bristol. She says, 'Many of the streets in the shopping centre are closed to traffic so that I can walk and shop in safety. Many cities have areas like this. They are called shopping precincts.

'You can see that trees have been planted and seats provided. This makes it a very attractive place to shop. I can buy many things here as there are all kinds of shops together in the one place.

'I like shopping in the big stores. There are a lot of these in the city centre. They are called department stores because the goods are arranged in different areas or departments. It's like a number of small shops all in the same building. The goods are displayed on large counters and taken to the cash desk to be paid for. You can take your time over choosing what you wish to buy. You don't have to queue at each counter.'

Look at the plan of part of Broadmead shopping centre.

1 Find the shopping streets which are closed to cars.
2 Find two places where shoppers can park their cars.
3 Find a danger spot for shoppers returning to their cars.
4 How are goods delivered to the shops in the precinct?

Broadmead shopping centre

Department store

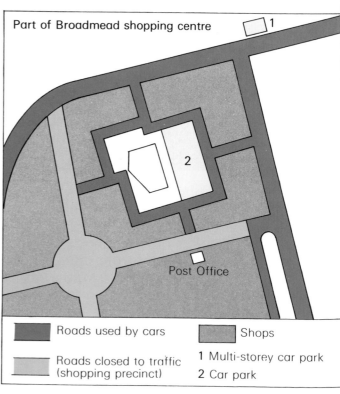

Part of Broadmead shopping centre

1 Multi-storey car park

2 Car park

Post Office

Roads used by cars

Shops

Roads closed to traffic (shopping precinct)

1 Multi-storey car park
2 Car park

The hypermarket

'These shops do not have as great a variety of goods as those in the shopping centre and prices are higher. But if I forget anything or need something in a hurry, they are very close at hand.'

The hypermarket

A new type of store called a hypermarket has been built recently on the outskirts of the city. This is a very large store selling many kinds of goods, such as groceries, hardware, clothes, etc.

Susan Brown goes there in the car and does a week's shopping in one trip. There is a very large free car park. She can push her shopping trolley right out to the car. Because the hypermarket is on the edge of the city shoppers avoid the heavy traffic of the city centre. The hypermarket is open till late in the evening. Prices are usually cheaper than in the other shops.

Copy the chart below and fill in the spaces to compare shopping in the three places. Where would you prefer to shop? Why?

Design a modern shopping centre for a city. Draw a plan of it. Remember to include precincts to separate cars from shoppers, car parks, things to make the area attractive to shoppers (trees, seats) and different types of shop.

The Browns' local shops

Local shops

The picture shows some shops near the Browns' flat. Susan Brown says, 'During the week I use the shops near the flats. The shopkeepers all know me and can guess what I want almost before I ask for it. I usually meet someone I know in the shops and we have time for a good chat.

	Broadmead Shopping Centre	Shops near the flat	Hypermarket
Good points			
Bad points			
When would you shop (day, time)?			

Section through a city

'I was 10 years old last week. For my birthday party Mum made me this birthday cake. When we had eaten half the cake, the side view looked like this. It is called a section through the cake.'

Look at the two views of Laura's birthday cake. Draw a plan of the whole cake.

Section through Bristol

Suburbs | Flats | Inner ring road

These are the outskirts of the city. This is where the hypermarket has been built.

Many old houses have been pulled down and the areas rebuilt with high blocks of flats.

This takes cars round the city centre and helps to prevent traffic jams in the centre itself.

This is a view of part of the city centre. What are the modern buildings used for? Which old buildings are still there? On the left of the picture is an area of open space. What might it be used for?

As a city grows, different buildings are added at different times. How many different ages of building are shown in the photograph?

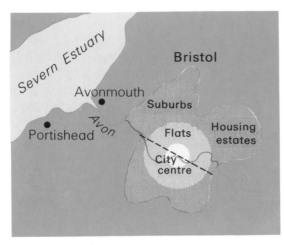

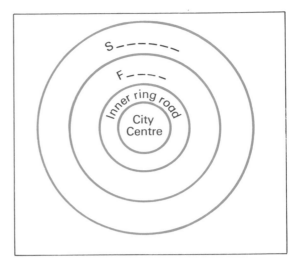

If we could cut a section through Bristol as we did with Laura's cake, it would look like the picture below. Look at the map of Bristol to see the line of the section through the city.

This is a target plan of Bristol. It shows the different regions of the city which you can see on the section. Copy the plan and complete the names in the rings.

City centre

Inner ring road

Flats

Suburbs

The houses and factories which were in the centre of Bristol have been pulled down.

Offices, shops, cinemas and hotels have been built in their place.

Many housing estates have been built in the suburbs to house new people coming into the area.

This is the Corn Exchange where business was conducted in Bristol for many years. Money was paid for goods by placing it on top of the pedestals which you can see in front of the building. They are known as 'nails'. Hence the expression 'paying on the nail'.

This is one of the cinemas in Bristol. Name two other kinds of entertainment which you might find in the centre of a city.

Look back at all the pictures of Bristol in this unit. Choose the most suitable words from this list to describe the city: old, new, busy, clean, crowded, peaceful, dull, lively, boring, dirty, modern.

Checking

Thinking

1   Why do people choose to live in cities? Pick out possible reasons from the following list: plenty of jobs, fresh air, good shopping, choice of entertainment, peace and quiet, traffic-free roads, good housing, lots of things to do and see. Can you add any other reasons?

Flat 2	Stairs	Lift	Flat 3
Flat 1			Flat 4
			Flat 5
Flat 7		Flat 6	

2   This is a plan of the ground floor of a block of flats. How many flats are there if the block is twelve storeys high? About how many houses would fit on the same piece of ground? List the advantages and disadvantages of living in a high-rise block of flats.

3   Read these sentences and copy the ones you think are true.
Land in the centre of cities is very expensive.
Not many firms want to build offices in the city centre.
Offices are pulled down to make room for small houses.
The outlying districts of a city are called suburbs.
A shopping precinct is full of cars.
A hypermarket is a large store selling many types of goods and is usually situated on the outskirts of a city.

There are many large department stores on the outskirts of a city. The city centre contains tall office blocks, large shops, hotels, theatres and cinemas.

British cities

Look at an atlas and find the names of the cities numbered on the map below.

Talking

Tell your friend about a favourite city you have visited. Talk about the shops, office blocks, flats, traffic, number of people and the noise. Did you travel about on foot, by car, by bus or by tube? What important places did you see? What did you like? What did you dislike? Would you rather live in a city or the country?

Doing

1 Draw the plan of Anycity, making it exactly twice the size. Mark on it where you would find the following:
the inner ring of high-rise flats,
the suburbs,
a good place to build a hypermarket,
a tall office block,
a large cinema.
Which part of the city would you like to live in? Why?

2 Bristol is both a city and a port. How many other cities do you know which are also ports? Check your answers in an atlas.

3 Look at the following pictures of cities and match them to the maps.

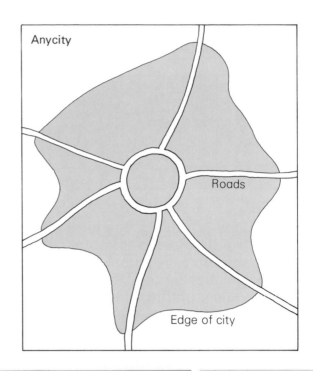

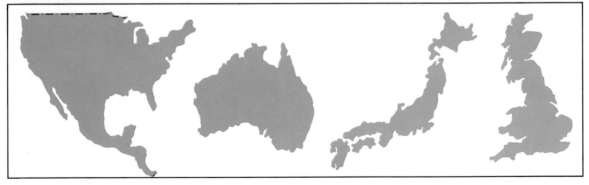

Going further

1 Plan a city centre. Start by drawing the main roads which come into the city. You could plan an inner ring road to prevent traffic jams in the centre. Include a shopping area, office areas, residential areas, recreation grounds, open spaces and places for entertainment. How will people cross the main roads in safety?

2 Look back at the section through Bristol. Draw a section through the city, town or village where you live. What is in the centre of your section? What is on the outskirts? How does it compare with the section of Bristol?

41

The Chards move to Runcorn

David Chard   Helen Chard   Jonathan Chard

Today is moving day for the Chards. They are moving from the centre of Liverpool to Runcorn New Town, 22 kilometres away. David works as an engineer and his firm is moving to a new factory on one of the new industrial estates in Runcorn. Helen is pleased to be moving. She is looking forward to living in a modern house in the new town instead of a small flat in part of an old house in Liverpool.

'It will be much better for the baby in the new town. We will have our own garden and a modern bathroom and kitchen. It won't be as noisy as Liverpool, but I'll miss having Mum and the relations living nearby. Still, they'll be able to visit us at weekends. They've been very good helping us to move. I hope we can soon make some new friends in the new town.'

Follow the Chards' journey on the map. Which river did they cross before reaching Runcorn? They drove over the Silver Jubilee Bridge. The Manchester Ship Canal runs alongside the river there. In the picture at the bottom of the page you can see a cargo ship being guided along the canal by two tugboats. It is on its way from Manchester to Liverpool and the open sea. On which side of the bridge is Runcorn? The map will help you.

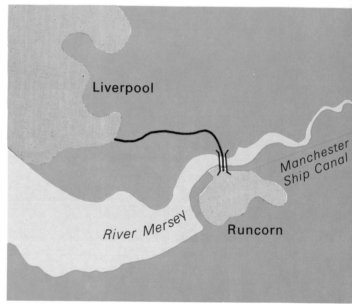

The Chards have moved into a house on the Palace Fields estate. Helen is very pleased with it. There is a lot more space and everything looks clean. There are trees and hedges near the houses. It is almost like living in the country.

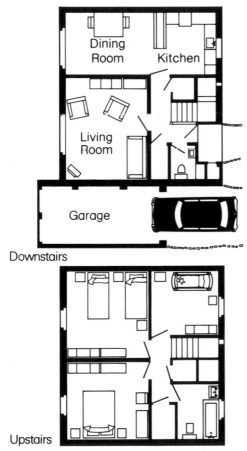

Downstairs

Upstairs

Here is a plan of the Chards' new house. How many rooms are there downstairs? How many bedrooms are there? The furniture is shown on the plans. What is there in the living room? Which is Jonathan's bedroom? Will the family's relations be able to stay overnight when they visit?

The house is in Badger Close. Find it on the plan of the estate. All the houses are on side roads joining Palace Fields Avenue which loops round the estate. Find the area of grass and woodland which runs through the centre of the estate. Footpaths cross this area, linking the houses to the school, the health centre, the church and local centre shops.

How would Helen Chard go shopping at the local centre if she went by car? How would she get there using the footpaths? Would it be quicker by car or on foot?

Follow these journeys on the plan. Helen Chard takes Jonathan to the health centre. Which route does she take? David visits new friends in Worthington Close. Which route does he take?

Make up some more journeys the Chards might make to visit different places on the estate.

A year later

The Chards have now lived in Runcorn for a year. This is what they said when they were asked what they thought about living in a new town.

What I like.
I don't have far to travel to work and a lot of my mates moved to Runcorn with me. The recreation centre is a great place to go. There's the chance to play lots of sports and you can meet new friends.

What I don't like.
All the buildings look the same. There aren't many old buildings in the new housing areas to give the place some character. Sometimes too much is provided for you. Everything seems to be run by the council. I miss the noise and bustle of Liverpool.

What I like
The house is very modern and easy to keep clean. There are lots of open spaces and grassy areas. The bus service is very good. The shops are all new and everything is together at Shopping City in the centre of town. There's no danger from cars in the pedestrian areas.

What I don't like.
I was rather lonely at first. None of my old friends and relatives were nearby to pop in for a cup of tea. I felt lost in the new town. It was like living on one piece of a jigsaw puzzle and not knowing how it fitted into the whole picture. There aren't many old people in the town and it seems strange without them.

Now I can walk, there are lots of safe places where I can play.

I don't see Gran and Grandad very often.

Shopping City

One place the whole family likes in Runcorn New Town is Shopping City. This is the new town centre which is within easy reach of all the housing estates. In this large covered area are shops, cafés, cinemas and a dance hall.

Town Square

In the middle of Shopping City is Town Square. Look at the photograph of Town Square. Everything is bright and colourful. It's a place where people can meet and talk. Helen Chard does her weekend shopping there. She can visit all the big stores and also shop in the arcade, an avenue of open shops rather like an old street market. What do you think Jonathan Chard likes to do in Town Square?

Exploring the town

During their first year in Runcorn the Chards explored the town. Here are some of the places they liked visiting.

The Sports Hall at Norton Recreation Centre

David comes here with some of his workmates. They play basketball during the week and have a football match every Saturday.

The Town Park

The park is in the middle of the new town. The Chards sometimes have a picnic here at weekends. It is only 1 kilometre from their house.

Halton Castle

The new town was built around Halton Hill with its ruined castle. From the top of the hill the Chards can see out over the Mersey estuary to Liverpool and their old home.

Runcorn New Town

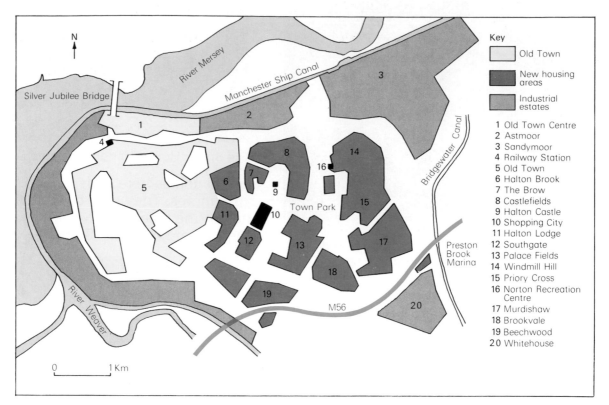

Key
- Old Town
- New housing areas
- Industrial estates

1 Old Town Centre
2 Astmoor
3 Sandymoor
4 Railway Station
5 Old Town
6 Halton Brook
7 The Brow
8 Castlefields
9 Halton Castle
10 Shopping City
11 Halton Lodge
12 Southgate
13 Palace Fields
14 Windmill Hill
15 Priory Cross
16 Norton Recreation Centre
17 Murdishaw
18 Brookvale
19 Beechwood
20 Whitehouse

This is a map of Runcorn New Town. Find Palace Fields estate where the Chards live. Find the following places visited by the family:

1 Shopping City
2 Norton Recreation Centre
3 The Town Park
4 Preston Brook Marina
5 Halton Castle

The new town was built around the old town of Runcorn and its surrounding villages. In between the housing areas are parks and woodland. There are three main parts to the new town: the old town, the new housing estates and the industrial estates. Find the three areas on the map.

Look at the graph showing the number of people in Runcorn in 1964. When the new town was built the number of people increased as families like the Chards moved into the town. More houses are being built. What is the expected population in 1981?

The new housing areas have been built to the east of the old town. Each area is like Palace Fields with its own shops, school and local centre within easy walking distance of the houses.

New industrial estates are situated away from the housing areas and near the motorway or the canals. Modern factories have been built for new firms to move into. David Chard's factory is on the Astmoor estate. These are some of the things made in the new factories: zip fasteners, beer, carpets, plastics, electrical goods, paint.

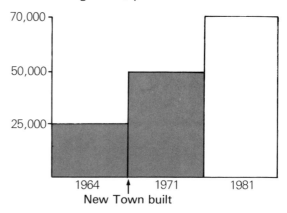

46

The busway

When the Chards visit Shopping City they travel by bus. Travelling by bus in Runcorn is much quicker and easier than in other towns. The buses have their own track or busway which loops round the town. It connects all the new housing areas with Shopping City, the industrial estates, the railway station and the secondary schools. No other vehicles are allowed on the busway and ordinary roads usually cross either over or under the track. The busway has been planned so that no house is more than five minutes' walking distance from a bus stop. Many people find it easier to use the bus instead of the car for town journeys. This helps to keep Runcorn free from traffic jams.

Below is a diagram to show the routes of the busway in Runcorn New Town. To make it simpler to use, the routes are shown in straight lines. Compare it with the map on the opposite page.

Find the routes used by the Chard family on the following journeys from Palace Fields estate:

Mr Chard — to Astmoor industrial estate to work; to Norton Recreation Centre to play football.
Mrs Chard — to Shopping City to buy clothes for Jonathan.
The Chard family — to the railway station to catch a train to Liverpool; to Windmill Hill estate to visit new friends.

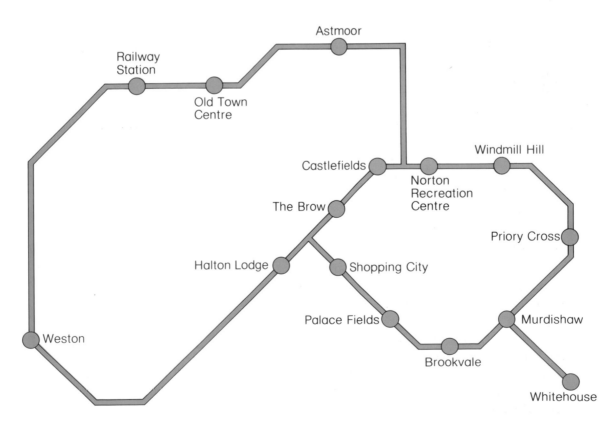

47

Checking

Thinking

1 Most of the cities in Britain are overcrowded. The map shows the new towns which have been built in Britain to house people from big cities.

The Chards moved to Runcorn to find a better home away from the crowded city of Liverpool.

1	Glenrothes
2	Cumbernauld
3	Irvine, Ayrshire
4	East Kilbride
5	Peterlee
6	Preston/Leyland/ Chorley
7	Skelmersdale
8	Warrington
9	Runcorn
10	Telford
11	Peterborough
12	Corby
13	Redditch
14	Milton Keynes
15	Cwmbran
16	Stevenage
17	Harlow
18	Basildon
19	Bracknell
20	Crawley

Look at the map. Which other new towns have been built to house people from Liverpool? Which new towns will house people from Glasgow? Which cities have people come from to live in the following new towns: Harlow, Cwmbran, Peterlee? Why are there no new towns in the north of Scotland or in the south west of England? Which is the nearest new town to your home? You will need an atlas.

2 There are many families like the Chards living on Palace Fields estate. Why do so few old people live there?

3 Look at all the pictures of Runcorn New Town. Find each place on the map on page 46.

Spotting shapes

This is the plan of one of the important buildings in Runcorn New Town. Which building is it? Look back at the pictures to help you.

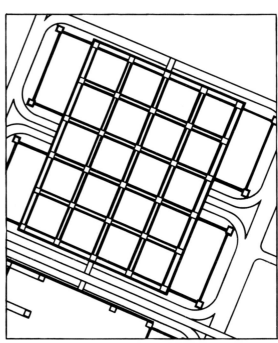

Doing

Design a house for a new town. Decide how many people are going to live in the house. Draw the front view of the house. Then draw plans for upstairs and downstairs.

Going further

1 Many people feel lonely when they first move to a new town. Write down some reasons for this. If you were a member of the new town council, what would you suggest to stop people feeling lonely?

2 Plan a new town. Make a copy of the outline map which shows the site for a new town. Draw the different parts of the new town on a separate piece of paper and cut them out. Decide where to place each part on the outline map. Remember to leave some areas clear for parks and recreation. Try not to mix industrial areas with housing areas.

When you have decided on the best arrangement, stick the parts down. Add a road system or busway to connect the different parts of the town.

Think of a name for your new town and name the different estates. Add any other details which would make your town an interesting place to live.

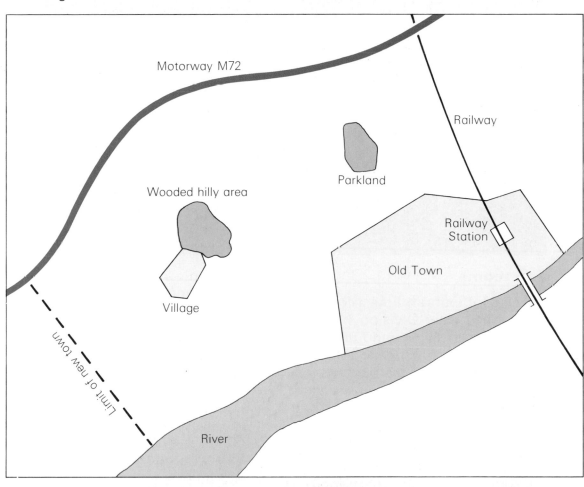

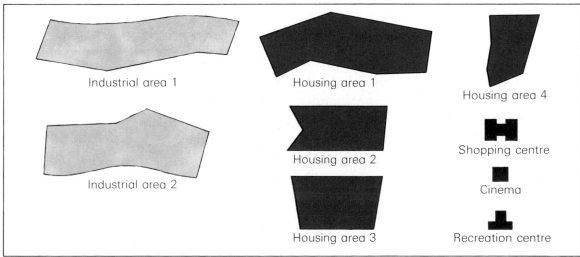

Toe to toe

Top team

This is Nottingham Forest football team. They were Division 1 champions in 1978 and European Cup champions in 1979. Some of the team members also played for England. They were Trevor Francis, Peter Shilton, Tony Woodcock and Viv Anderson.

The league table shows how many games the team played in 1978 and how many they won or lost. The table also shows all the other teams they played during the season. How many games did Nottingham Forest play? How many did they win? Which team do you support? Is it mentioned in the table? How many games did it win?

The Nottingham Forest team has to do a lot of travelling during the season. Look at the league table again to find out where the team goes. Some cities or areas have more than one team.

London – Arsenal, Chelsea, Queens Park Rangers, West Ham.
Midlands – West Bromwich Albion, Aston Villa, Wolves.
Liverpool – Liverpool, Everton.
Manchester – Manchester United, Manchester City.

Use an atlas to find the team furthest away from Nottingham Forest. How far do the players have to travel for an away match with this team?

FIRST DIVISION

		Home			Goals			Away			Goals		
	P	W	D	L	F	A	W	D	L	F	A	Pts
Nottm. F. ...	42	15	6	0	37	8	10	8	3	32	16	64
Liverpool	42	15	4	2	37	11	9	5	7	28	23	57
Everton	42	14	4	3	47	22	8	7	6	29	23	55
Man. City ...	42	14	4	3	46	21	6	8	7	28	30	52
Arsenal	42	14	5	2	38	12	7	5	9	22	25	52
W.B.A.	42	14	5	3	35	18	5	9	7	27	35	50
Coventry	42	13	5	3	48	23	5	7	9	27	39	48
Aston Villa ..	42	11	6	4	33	18	7	6	8	24	24	46
Leeds Utd. ..	42	12	4	5	39	21	6	6	9	24	32	46
Man. Utd. ..	42	9	6	6	32	23	7	4	10	35	40	42
Birmingham .	42	8	5	8	32	30	8	4	9	23	30	41
Derby Co. ...	42	10	7	4	37	24	1	10	10	24	46	40
Norwich	42	10	8	3	28	20	1	10	10	24	46	40
Middlesbro .	42	8	8	5	25	19	4	7	10	17	35	39
Wolves	42	7	8	6	30	27	5	4	12	21	37	36
Chelsea	42	7	11	3	28	20	3	3	14	18	49	36
Bristol City .	42	9	6	6	37	26	2	7	12	12	27	35
Ipswich	42	10	5	6	32	24	1	8	12	15	37	35
Q.P.R. :.....	42	8	8	5	27	26	1	7	13	20	38	33
West Ham ...	42	8	6	7	31	28	4	2	15	21	41	32
Newcastle ...	42	4	6	11	26	37	2	4	15	16	41	22
Leicester ...	42	4	7	10	16	32	1	5	15	10	38	22

LEAGUE CUP & CHAMPIONSHIP

Double for Notts Forest

CLOUGH'S GLORY BOYS

Kings of the Forest

These newspaper headlines show what some people think about the team. On Saturday afternoons in the vicinity of City Ground, where Forest play, there may be other opinions.

What would you say if you lived near the ground?

Playing away

Nottingham Forest are drawn against Manchester United. They are playing away from home at Manchester United's ground, Old Trafford. The team travels by coach on the route shown on the map.

Which roads does the coach take? How many kilometres does the coach travel? Which hills does the coach cross? How far is it from Nottingham to Sheffield?

Many of the team's supporters travel along the same route. Long before the game starts, the ground at Old Trafford begins to fill with spectators. The Manchester United supporters stay behind the goal at the Stretford end. Nottingham Forest's supporters are mainly at the opposite end of the ground. The pitch is a boundary between the two rival sets of supporters. Find other boundaries marked on the pitch. What are they?

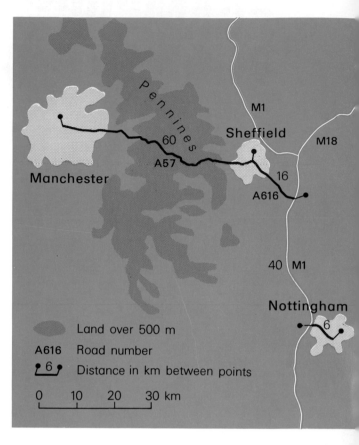

Goal!

Opposite is a plan of the move which ended in the only goal of the match. O'Neill took the free kick. He curved the ball round the wall of players. Francis ran forward and hit the ball into the back of the net.

Final score: Manchester United 0, Nottingham Forest 1.

52

Spot the ball

Here is a picture taken during a match. Where do you think the ball should be?

If you use the numbers on the edges of the picture you can name the square where the ball should be. Use the E lines before the N lines. You can remember this because E comes before N in the alphabet.

The head of the player on the right is in square E8N5. Now, where's the ball? The answer is at the bottom of the page.

Some maps also have lines and numbers to help you pinpoint places. Look at the map below. In which square is (a) the football ground; (b) the motorway junction? What is there (a) in square E8N3; (b) in square E5N5? The answers are at the bottom of the page.

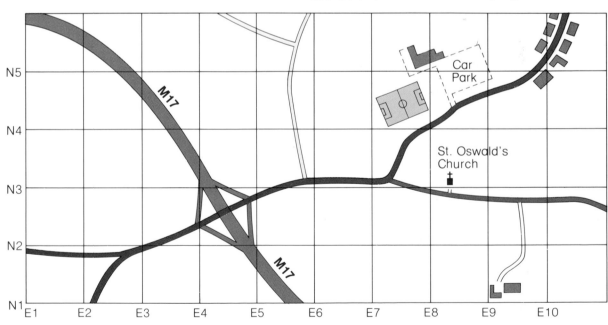

Answers

The ball is in square E9N1.

The football ground is in square E7N4.

The motorway junction is in square E4N2.

In square E8N3 is St Oswald's Church.

In square E5N5 there is a road junction.

Championships

The European Cup

The best teams from each country in Europe play one another in a knock-out competition. The winner of the final receives the European Cup.

During the competition the teams travel to many different countries in Europe. The map below shows some of those countries. It also shows the journeys made by Nottingham Forest and their supporters for the 1979 European Cup final. The match was played in Munich in West Germany. Nottingham Forest won the game against Malmo, a team from Sweden.

The team and some supporters went by air. The journey took 2 hours and cost £210 each.
The supporters who went by train–boat–train took 10 hours. It cost £160 each.

The supporters who went by coach–boat–coach took 14 hours. It cost £100 each.
The supporters who went by car–ferry–car took 12 hours. It cost £70 each.
Which journey took the shortest time? Which journey was the cheapest? Which of the journeys would you like to make?

Find Malmo on the map. Who had the shortest distance to travel, Nottingham Forest supporters or Malmo supporters?

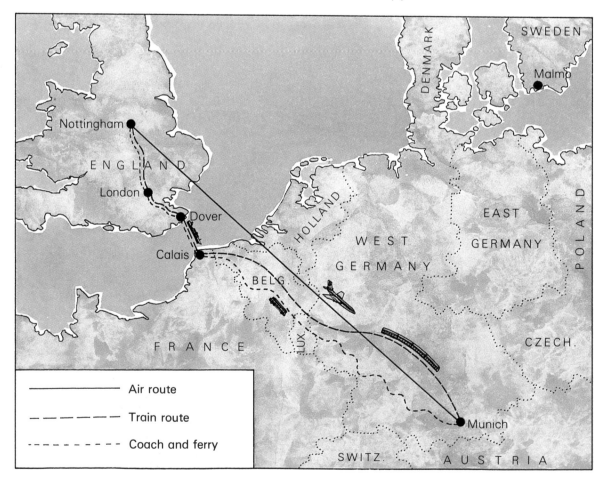

Air route

Train route

Coach and ferry

The World Cup

Every four years the footballing countries of the world take part in a competition to see which country has the best team. In 1978 the World Cup competition was held in Argentina. In the final, Argentina beat Holland by 3 goals to 1.

TV pictures of the matches were sent by satellite to Britain. This meant that we could watch the matches 'live' as they were being played.

Look at the picture of the earth. The earth spins on its axis in the direction shown by the pink arrows. The part of the earth facing the sun is in sunlight. There it is daytime. The part of the earth facing away from the sun is in shadow. There it is night.

It takes 24 hours for the earth to spin round on its axis. During that time, each place on the earth's surface will have a night and a day as it moves into the shadow and then comes round into the sunlight again. Find Argentina and Britain on the picture. Which country is moving into the shadow for night?

Because countries have day and night at different times, their clocks will read different times. What time is it in Britain on the picture? What time is it in Argentina?

The time difference between the two countries is four hours. When it is afternoon in Argentina, it is early evening in Britain. The World Cup final was played at 3.00 p.m. in Argentina but it was seen 'live' on TV in Britain at 7.00 p.m.

The 1980 Olympic Games were held in Moscow, in Russia. 'Live' TV pictures were sent to Britain. Look at the picture of the earth again and find Moscow. The time difference between Moscow and Britain is two hours. When it is early afternoon in Moscow, it is late morning in Britain. If a race took place in the Moscow Olympics at 2.00 p.m. what time could we have seen it 'live' on TV in Britain?

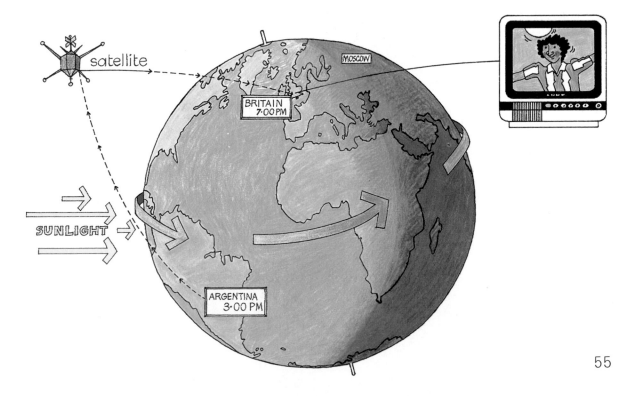

Checking

Doing

1 Use an atlas to help you draw a map of England to show the cities which have football teams in the First Division. Can you name any of their grounds?

2 Draw a map of Europe to show the following places which have famous football teams:
Hamburg – Hamburg SV
Madrid – Real Madrid
Milan – Inter Milan
Zurich – Grasshopper Zurich
Moscow – Dynamo
Munich – Bayern Munich
Bruges – FC Bruges
Munchen Gladbach – Borussia MG
Belgrade – Red Star
Amsterdam – Ajax
Name the countries in which each city is found.

Talking

Everyone is worried about the increase in violence amongst spectators at football matches. Talk with a friend about ways of stopping the violence. What causes the violence? Would you improve the football grounds? Would you separate rival supporters? How would you punish offenders?

Going further

1 Soccer has recently become very popular in North America. The teams from the USA and Canada have very colourful names with team badges to match. Some are shown above. The badges tell you something about the places the teams represent.

Look at the badges and write a sentence to say what they tell you about California, Detroit, Portland, San José and Washington.

2 The map shows all the cities with teams in the North American Soccer League. The names of the teams are shown below the map.

Make a copy of the map. Using an atlas to help you, write the name of each team in the correct place on the map. Three of the teams are in Canada. Which are they?

3 The distance across North America from the west coast to the east coast is 4,000 kilometres. Because the distance is so great, there is a time difference of 3 hours between the coasts.

If a match is played at the ground of the Los Angeles Aztecs at 3.00 p.m. and the game is relayed by satellite, what time would it be seen 'live' on TV in New York?

What time would a viewer in San Francisco see a 'live' telecast of a game played at 2.00 p.m. at the ground of the New York Cosmos?

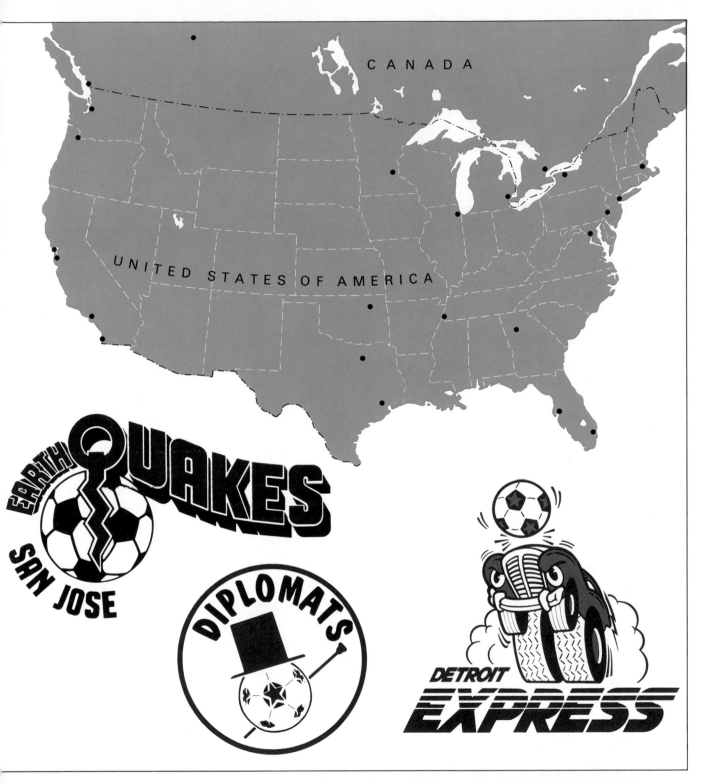

New York Cosmos
Washington Diplomats
Toronto Blizzard
Rochester Lancers
Minnesota Kicks
Tulsa Roughnecks
Dallas Tornadoes
Atlanta Chiefs

Vancouver Whitecaps
Los Angeles Aztecs
Portland Timbers
Seattle Sounders
Tampa Bay Rowdies
Fort Lauderdale Strikers
New Engand Teamen
Philadelphia Fury

Houston Hurricane
Chicago Sting
Detroit Express
Memphis Rogues
San Diego Sockers
Edmonton Drillers
San Jose Earthquakes
California Surf

Moving goods

Bill McBain is a long distance lorry driver. He lives in Glasgow but most of the time he is away from home driving his lorry. He drives goods from factories in Britain to customers all over Europe. As it is the school holidays, Bill is taking his son Robert with him. Today's load is a container full of Scotch whisky for Milan in Italy.

Robert is very excited. He is looking forward to his journey across Europe. He has worked out the route from his father's book of road maps and has copied it on to a piece of paper. He has marked the main towns they have to pass through and has worked out the distances in kilometres. He has also marked the rivers and ranges of hills they have to cross. Check Robert's map by looking at an atlas.

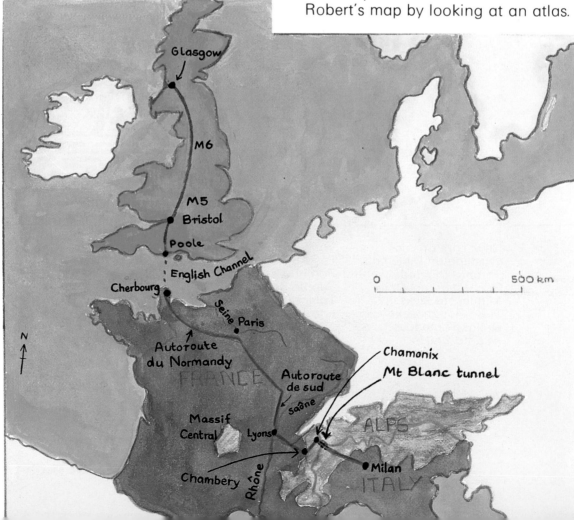

Before they set off, Robert makes a note of the time and the number of kilometres shown on the lorry's dashboard. Now he will be able to time the journey and check the distances.

The first part of the journey is along motorways. Bill has a compass in his cab. By looking at the compass Robert can see that they are travelling south.

Bill drives the lorry down the M6 and M5 motorways. Other lorries are travelling in the same direction. Robert notices how the drivers flash their lights to each other to signal when it is safe to overtake.

Eventually they arrive at Poole, a port on the south coast of England. As they drive into the dock area, Robert sees a signpost pointing out to sea. It shows the distance across the English Channel to the French port of Cherbourg. The lorry is driven on to a ship waiting at the quayside.

Bill is driving his lorry all the way to Milan. Other lorries are having their containers removed and loaded on to a different ship. The containers will be transferred to French lorries when they arrive in Cherbourg.

Before getting out of the lorry to explore the ship, Robert looks at the kilometre reading on the dashboard and notes the time.

How far has the lorry travelled from Glasgow to Poole? How long has it taken?

Crossing the Channel

Bill and Robert are sailing across the Channel on the **M.V. Coutances.** Part of the ship's side has been cut away in the picture so that you can see where the lorries are parked. There is room for 48 lorries on board the ship. 50 cars are parked on the bottom two decks. Some are going to customers in Europe.

Robert enjoys looking round the ship. He watches the lorries being chained down so that they will not move if there is rough weather on the voyage.

Explore the rest of the ship with Robert. Follow his path on the cut-away picture. Here is a list of the places he visits:

Cafeteria – he has a lemonade.
Bows (front) of the ship
Bridge – the captain shows him the ship's controls.

Top deck – he looks at the radar and radio masts.
Lifeboat – he examines the hoists that are holding up the boat.
Upper deck – he looks at the lorries.
Stern (back) of the ship
Sleeping quarters – he returns to his cabin which is sixth from the left. He is sitting on the bottom right-hand bunk.
Look at the map on page 61. It shows some of the ferry routes across the Channel between England and France. Find the route taken by the **M.V. Coutances.** Complete the following cross-channel links by copying out the list and inserting the missing ports.

Poole – Cherbourg
Newhaven –
Folkestone –
– Calais

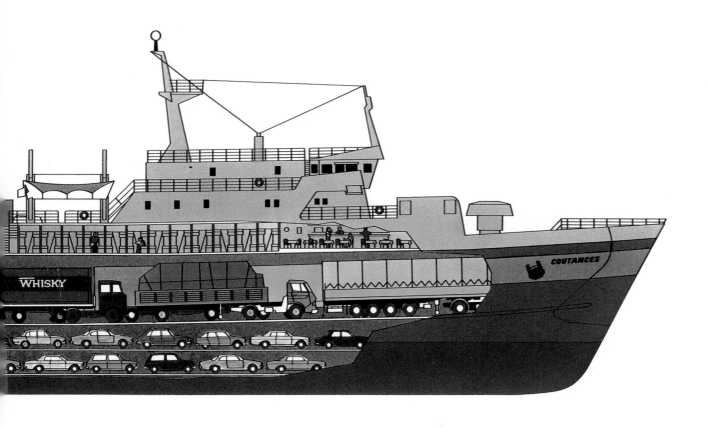

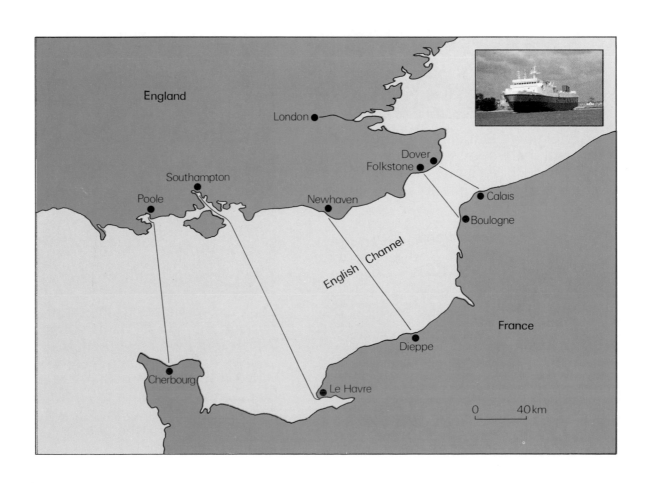

Across Europe

The **M.V. Coutances** arrives in Cherbourg early the following morning. Bill drives the lorry off the ship on to the quayside. While the French customs officers check the lorry to see if the load is correct, Robert looks at the kilometre reading. Why is it the same as when the lorry left Poole?

3 5 7 6 0 km

Soon the lorry is on its way across France. Check the route with the map on page 58. Most of the journey is along autoroutes. These are French motorways. Bill has to pay a toll to travel on the autoroutes. The money helps to pay for the upkeep of the roads.

At lunchtime Bill drives off the autoroute and stops at a building which has this sign.

Bill knows that he can get a good meal there at a reasonable price. This is Robert's first meal in France. Look at the picture to see what he has to eat.

French Bread
Carafe of water.
Salad.
Camembert Cheese
Pâté.

After lunch they drive along the autoroute du sud. Robert looks at the compass. 'We're driving south so autoroute du sud must mean motorway of the south', he says. 'That's right', says Bill.

Crossing the Alps

At Lyons they leave the autoroute and turn east towards the Alps, a range of snow-capped mountains between France and Italy. When they reached Chambery, Bill has to decide which route to take across the Alps.

They can either drive over the Mount Cenis pass which is a long climb with many hairpin bends and a steep descent on the other side. Or they can go through the Mont Blanc tunnel.

Look at the picture of the road through the Mount Cenis pass. Which route would you choose if you were driving a heavy lorry? Why? If it was winter there would be no choice because the pass is closed from November until April. Why do you think the pass is closed in winter?

The picture shows the car suspended on the cable. Far below Robert can see the small figures of skiers moving down the slopes. To one side of the cable car he can see an ice-filled valley, or glacier, glinting in the sunlight. On the other side he can see sharp mountain peaks. These are the Aiguilles. It is a well-chosen name. Find out what the French word 'aiguille' means. The cable car seems very small in this vast and awe-inspiring landscape.

Robert rejoins Bill at Entreve on the Italian side of the mountains. They are soon on the last lap of their journey along the Italian motorway, or autostrada, to Milan.

Milan is the end of the journey. There the lorry is unloaded at a warehouse and the crates of whisky are stored ready to be sent all over Italy. Robert checks the dashboard reading for the last time. Bill is arranging to take back a load of tinned tomatoes to Scotland.

Bill decides to go through the tunnel. They spend the night in Chamonix, a winter sports town on the French side of the tunnel. Next morning Bill has a surprise for Robert. He has bought him a ticket to travel on the cable car route over the mountains. Bill will drive through the tunnel and wait for Robert on the Italian side.

The map shows both journeys across the Alps. Robert's cable car journey takes him high into the mountains. The views are breathtaking. The air is clear and the snow-covered peaks stand out sharply against the blue sky.

3 7 0 2 3 km

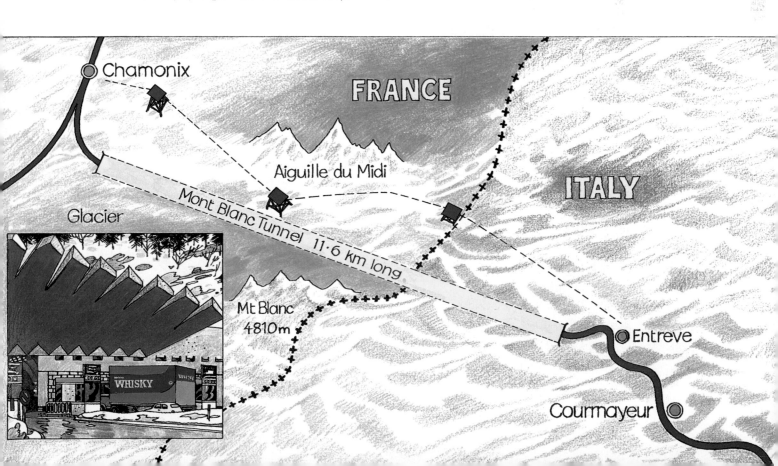

Checking

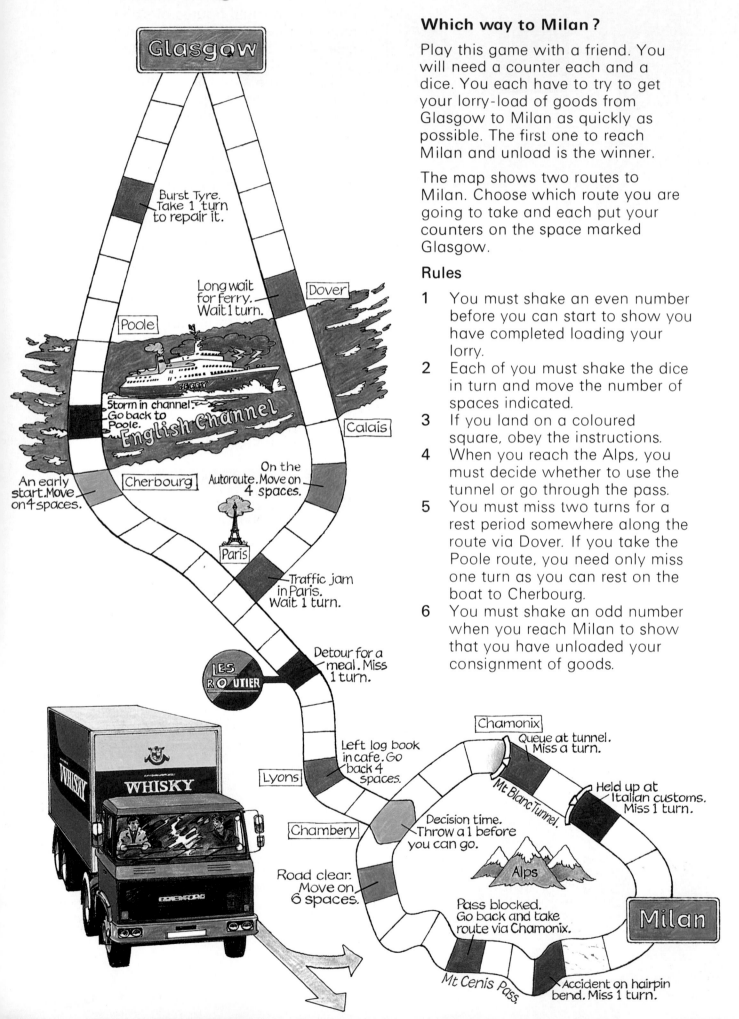

Which way to Milan?

Play this game with a friend. You will need a counter each and a dice. You each have to try to get your lorry-load of goods from Glasgow to Milan as quickly as possible. The first one to reach Milan and unload is the winner.

The map shows two routes to Milan. Choose which route you are going to take and each put your counters on the space marked Glasgow.

Rules

1　You must shake an even number before you can start to show you have completed loading your lorry.
2　Each of you must shake the dice in turn and move the number of spaces indicated.
3　If you land on a coloured square, obey the instructions.
4　When you reach the Alps, you must decide whether to use the tunnel or go through the pass.
5　You must miss two turns for a rest period somewhere along the route via Dover. If you take the Poole route, you need only miss one turn as you can rest on the boat to Cherbourg.
6　You must shake an odd number when you reach Milan to show that you have unloaded your consignment of goods.

Glasgow

Burst Tyre. Take 1 turn to repair it.

Long wait for ferry. Wait 1 turn.

Dover

Poole

Storm in channel. Go back to Poole.

English Channel

Calais

An early start. Move on 4 spaces.

Cherbourg

On the Autoroute. Move on 4 spaces.

Paris

Traffic jam in Paris. Wait 1 turn.

LES ROUTIER

Detour for a meal. Miss 1 turn.

Chamonix

Queue at tunnel. Miss a turn.

Left log book in cafe. Go back 4 spaces.

Lyons

Mt Blanc Tunnel.

Held up at Italian customs. Miss 1 turn.

WHISKY

Chambery

Decision time. Throw a 1 before you can go.

Alps

Road clear. Move on 6 spaces.

Pass blocked. Go back and take route via Chamonix.

Milan

Mt Cenis Pass

Accident on hairpin bend. Miss 1 turn.

	Km reading	distance travelled
Glasgow	35050	Km
Poole		
Poole to Cherbourg	by ferry	Km
Cherbourg		Km
Milan		
Total distance for journey		Km

Thinking

1   Robert kept a record of the distance travelled on the journey from Glasgow to Milan. Here is his chart. Copy it out and fill in the missing spaces. Add together the number of kilometres travelled on each stage of the journey to find the total distance from Glasgow to Milan.

How long did the journey take? Name the two places where Robert and Bill spent the night on the journey.

2   Copy this compass chart and fill in the missing directions.

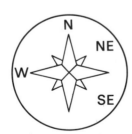

Look back at Robert's map on page 58. In which direction was the lorry travelling on the following stretches of the journey?

Glasgow to Poole
Cherbourg to Paris
Paris to Chambery
Chambery to Chamonix
Chamonix to Milan

3   Look back over the unit to find the answers to these questions. How far is it from Dover to Calais? In which country is Glasgow? In which country is Milan? How long is the Mont Blanc tunnel? How high is Mont Blanc? Where does Bill stop for the Italian customs men to check his lorry?

Doing

Make a model of either Bill's lorry or the **M.V. Coutances**. Use cardboard boxes, tubes, empty plastic bottles and any other suitable things you can find.

Going further

1   Design a ferry which will take lorries across the Channel. Draw a cut-away section to show the different decks of the ship.

2   Use an atlas to help you plan a journey across Europe from Manchester to Madrid in Spain.

3   Make a model of a scene in the Alps. Paint a mountain scene to go behind the model. Include a cable car, a glacier, skiers, hairpin bends and a tunnel through the mountains.

Commuters

This is a picture of one of the main roads leading into London. The time is 8.30 a.m. on a weekday. People are driving into the city on their way to work.

Because so many people are travelling at the same time there are long traffic jams. The roads are full of cars and buses and it takes a long time to travel a short distance. In the evening the cars will all be travelling in the opposite direction taking people home.

The times of day when people travel into the city to work or out of the city on their way home are known as the rush hours.

Many people travel by train to work. During the morning rush hour the trains into the city are full. People have to stand. There are long queues at the station.

People who travel long distances every morning to get to work and every evening to get home are known as commuters. The trains which take them into the city are called commuter trains. Look at the map of London showing all the roads and railways which lead into the city. Imagine the roads full of cars all travelling into the city every morning. No wonder there are traffic jams.

London is not the only city to have a commuter problem. Many cities all over the world face the same problem.

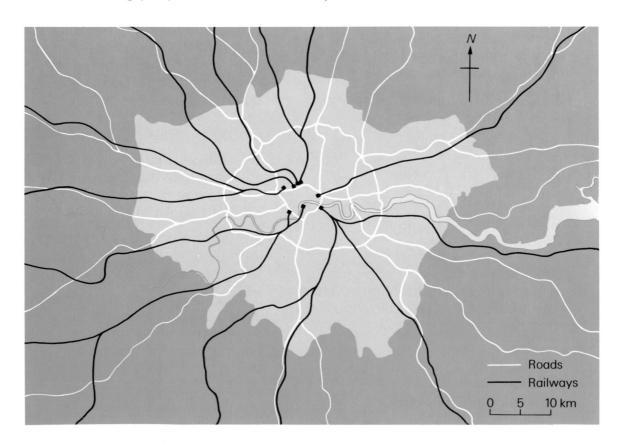

N

Roads
Railways
0   5   10 km

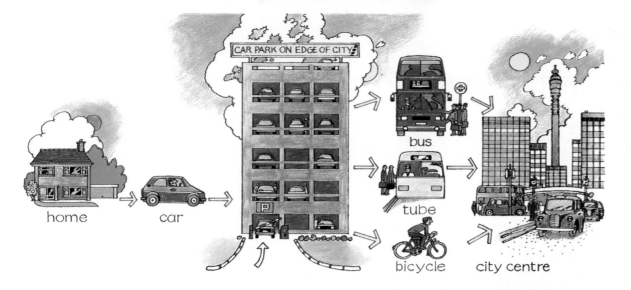

home   car   CAR PARK ON EDGE OF CITY   bus   tube   bicycle   city centre

Once the car commuters reach the city centre there is the problem of finding a place to park. Many commuters now park their cars in large car parks on the outskirts of the city and travel the rest of the way by other methods.

Travelling by bus means having to wait in queues.

Travelling by tube means travelling on packed trains. In Tokyo students are given the job of pushing passengers into the trains. Sometimes the pushers are also pushed in by mistake.

This man has a folding bike in his boot. He can ride through the traffic jams, but he'll get wet when it rains.

In Japan many people cycle to the railway stations and travel into the cities by train. They leave their bicycles in a large heap and collect any bike from the heap on their way home.

That's mine right in the middle!

STATION

67

Why commute?

Look back at pages 38 and 39. Find the suburbs of Bristol. They are in a ring round the city. Most people live in the suburbs and have to travel into the centre of the city for their work. They prefer to live on the outskirts of the city because the houses there are not crowded together. They are also nearer the countryside.

Some people have moved from cities to live in smaller towns around the city boundary. People spend most of their day away from these towns, working in the city, and only return to them in the evening.

The towns are called dormitory towns. What is a dormitory? The French word 'dormir' means to sleep.

A commuter's timetable

Below is a diagram of a commuter's timetable. How much time is spent travelling each day? How long is the commuter away from home? How long is spent at home? Think of your own day. Draw a timetable similar to the one below to show your day. Mark in the important times. What do you do in the evenings? Mark it on the timetable.

Get up… | leave home… | catch train… | arrive in city… | arrive at work… | work…

work… | leave work… | queue at station… | catch train… | arrive at station… | arrive home.

With faster train services people can live further away from cities and still commute every day. Inter-city trains now link many distant places with London. This is an inter-city 125 train. It is a high speed train which runs on certain routes to London. Why is it called 125?

Time by train to London

The map shows places which are less than two hours away from London by inter-city 125 trains. To show this clearly, the map has been simplified. The distances and scale are not correct but the stations are in the right order and roughly in the right directions. The routes used by the 125 trains are shown in red.

Look at the map and answer the questions.

1 Commuters rarely want to travel for more than $1\frac{1}{2}$ hours to work. Most commuters travel for even less time. Name the stations on each route which mark the limit of $1\frac{1}{2}$ hours' travel to London.
2 Which Bristol station would you use for the fastest journey to London?
3 Compare the map with an atlas map showing southern England. Find the distances from Bristol to London and from Dover to London. Which is the greater distance? Why is the train journey quicker from Bristol?

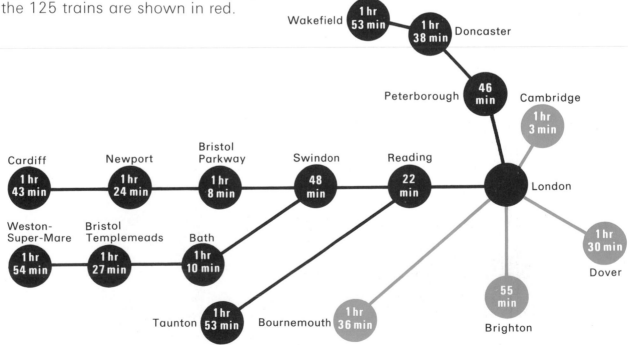

Travelling to school

Here is a diagram showing how children in class 4 travel to school.

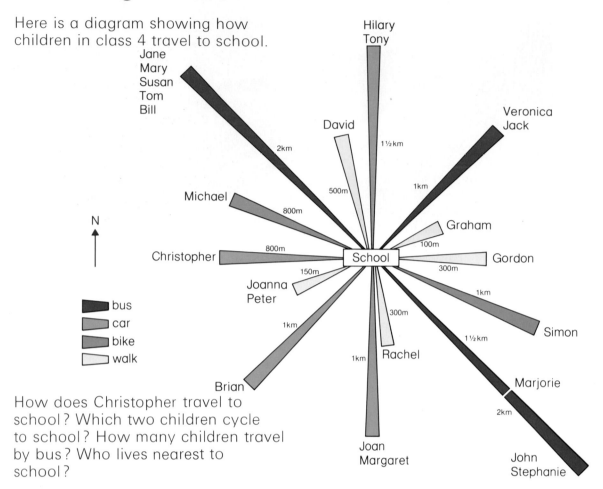

How does Christopher travel to school? Which two children cycle to school? How many children travel by bus? Who lives nearest to school?

The diagram also shows which direction the children come from. Look back at the compass directions on page 23. Who lives due north of the school? In which direction does Gordon live? Who lives 1 kilometre south west of the school? The bus travelling from the north west brings five children. Who are they?

By looking at the diagram Michael counted the number of different ways children travel to school. Then he made a chart to show how many children travel by car, by bus, by bicycle and on foot.

Here is the chart he made.

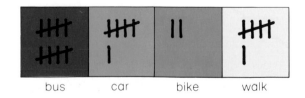

From this information he started to make a graph. He called it
Class 4 – journeys to school.
Michael has shown the information for bus and car journeys. Copy the graph and complete it by showing how many children cycle and walk to school. Make a similar graph for your own class.

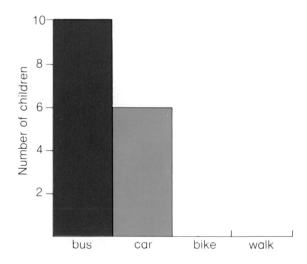

70

Checking

Thinking

1 Copy out the sentences below and insert the correct word in each gap from this list: dormitory towns, car parks, inter-city, bicycle, rush hour, tube, commuters, bus, home.

Every working day —— travel to work in the cities. During the —— the roads become jammed with traffic. The same thing happens in the evening when everyone is going —— to the —— outside the city. To solve the parking problem some commuters leave their cars in —— on the outskirts of the cities and travel the rest of the way by ——, —— or ——. Now that there are fast —— trains people can live further away from the cities where they work.

2 Small electric cars are being designed for use between car parks on the edge of the city and the city centre. How will they help (a) the parking problem in the city; (b) the pollution problem?

Can you think of any other advantages of electric cars?

Talking

Have you ever been stuck in a traffic jam? Talk to a friend about it. What did you feel like? How long were you stuck in the jam? How did the driver feel? Look at the picture on page 66. What is it like at rush hour? Talk about the people, the traffic, the noise and the smells.

Doing

Look back at the commuter's timetable on page 68. Make a copy of this 24-hour clock. Divide it up to show how the commuter spends his day. The time he spends sleeping is already marked for you on the clock. Draw another 24-hour clock to show how you spend your day.

Going further

Design a car for use in the city. It will be used by people who have parked their own cars on the outskirts of the city. They will use it to get to their offices or to go to the shops. It must be small and easy to park but there should be room for at least two people. It should have a quiet engine and must not add to the pollution of the city centre.

A class exercise

Collect or draw pictures of cars, buses, lorries and other vehicles. Make a frieze of a traffic jam.

Country lanes and motorways

The Chards of Runcorn decided to go on holiday to North Devon. Look at the holiday brochures they collected from the travel agent. Find Runcorn and the four holiday places on the map. Which of the four is not on the coast? Look back to the map on page 21. What kind of area is it? The picture on the brochure will help you.

The Chards drove to North Devon in their car. They wanted to use it for touring once they got to Devon.

Before they left Runcorn, David Chard studied the map and planned their route. They could use motorways for most of the journey.

Imagine you are David Chard planning the route. Look at the map and answer these questions.

1 Which motorways will you travel on?
2 Where will you leave the motorway and join an ordinary road?
3 How far is it from Runcorn to Clovelly?
4 How far will you travel by motorway?
5 How far will you travel by ordinary road?

David Chard made a simple line diagram of his route so that he could look at it as he drove instead of having to look at a map. Here is the start of his diagram. Copy it out and complete it.

Runcorn
M56
M6
M6
M5
M4
M5
T - - - - -   A - - -
B - - - - - - - - -
C - - - - - - - - -   A - -

Motorways
Other roads
0 20 40 60 80 100 km

72

The distance from Runcorn to Taunton is 336 kilometres. The Chards were able to travel very quickly along the motorway for this part of the journey. The speed of their car was 112 km.p.h.

Look at the graph below. The time taken is shown at the side of the graph. The distance travelled is shown along the bottom of the graph. How long did it take the Chards to travel 112 kilometres? You can find out by looking at point **A** on the journey line. It is 112 kilometres along the distance scale and 1 hour on the time scale. How long did it take the Chards to reach Taunton?

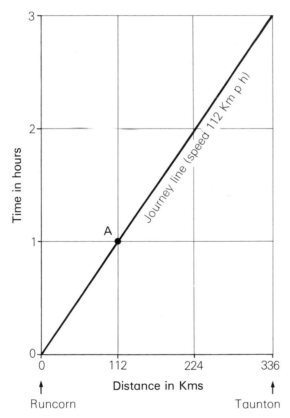

When the Chards left the motorway at Taunton they had to travel along ordinary roads. They were very winding and narrow compared with the motorway. David Chard could not drive very fast along these roads. It took 1½ hours to drive from Taunton to Barnstaple. Look at the map on the opposite page. What is the distance from Taunton to Barnstaple?

At Barnstaple there was a traffic jam because lots of other people were also travelling to the coast for a holiday. The car crawled from Barnstaple to Clovelly. It took another 1½ hours.

Look at the graph for this part of the journey. It shows that the slowest part of the journey was between Barnstaple and Clovelly.

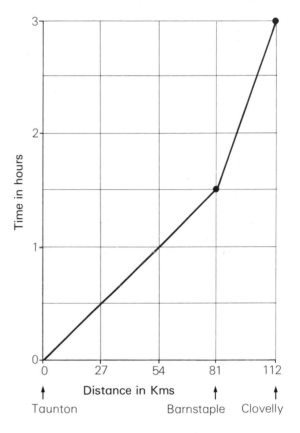

Copy the chart below and use the information on this page to complete it.

	Distance	Time
Runcorn to Taunton		
Taunton to Barnstaple		
Barnstaple to Clovelly		
Total for journey		

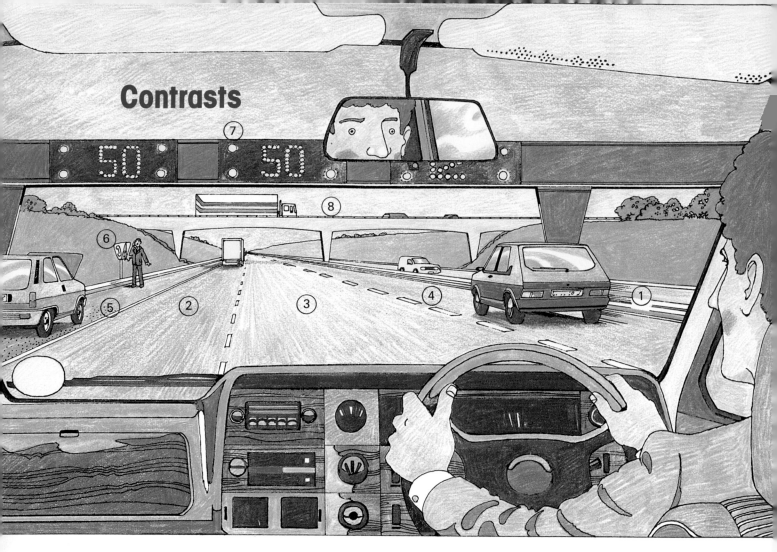

Contrasts

Motorway

Look for all these features next time you travel on a motorway.

1   Central reservation separating vehicles driving in opposite directions. Often there is a crash barrier to keep cars on their own side of the road if they go out of control.
2   Slow lane for lorries and slow-moving traffic.
3   Middle lane for faster moving traffic.
4   Overtaking lane.
5   Hard shoulder for use when a car breaks down so that it does not hold up the traffic.
6   Emergency telephone where a driver can telephone for help. There is a telephone every 1.6 km.
7   Flashing signals to give warning of dangers ahead.
8   Bridge carrying an ordinary road over the motorway to avoid crossroads on the motorway.

Motorway maze

Traffic changes from motorways to ordinary roads or other motorways at junctions or interchanges. How can the red car get to Y? How can the blue car get to Y? How can the green car get to X? How can the red car get to X? Find other routes for cars using this interchange.

Country lane

Look at the picture of a country lane. It shows some of the reasons why David Chard could not drive very quickly along this type of road. How many reasons can you find? Make a list of them. Here is one to start you off. The narrow road makes it difficult to pass oncoming traffic.

Some drivers prefer to travel on ordinary roads because they find motorways boring. Drivers need to concentrate hard on motorways because of the high speeds. The Chards liked using motorways to travel to North Devon because they could get there quickly They preferred country lanes when they were in Devon because the lanes were more interesting and the family could drive slowly and enjoy the countryside.

Spotting shapes

Here are some signs the Chards saw on their journey. Find out what each sign means and whether you would find it on a motorway or an ordinary road.

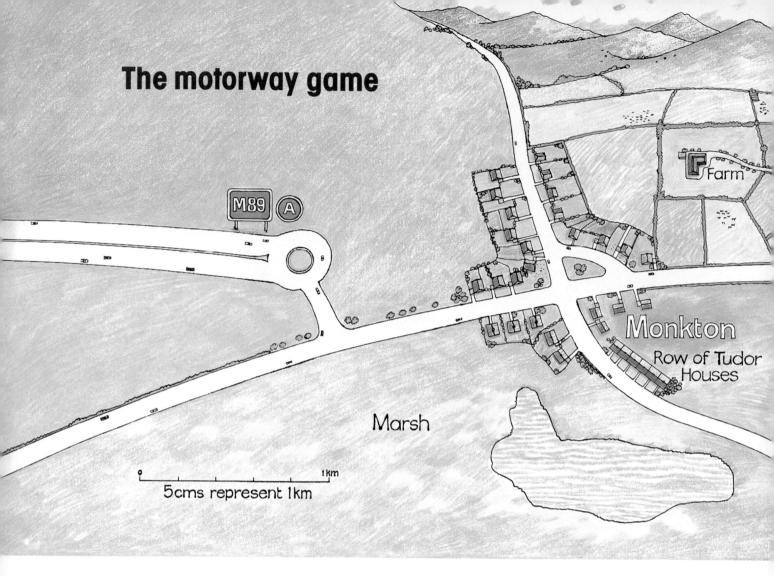

The motorway game

Part 1 Build a motorway

Look at the map. It shows an area of countryside near the small town of Monkton. The M89 motorway has to pass through this area. Which route would you plan for the motorway? Draw a copy of the map so that you can plan your route on it.

Rules

1 The motorway must join up with the two sections of the M89 shown at **A** and **B**.
2 The cost of the route must not be more than 150 units. Check your spending with the cost list below.
3 Your route must avoid upsetting people in the area wherever possible.
4 The hilly area shown to the north of the map cannot be used for your route. It would cost too much to level the ground.

When you have decided on the best route for the motorway, draw it clearly on your map ready to present to the motorway inquiry in Part 2 of the game. Add up the cost of your route.

Cost list

Cost of building 1 kilometre of motorway — 10 units.
Cost of building a bridge or a viaduct — 10 units.
Cost of a cattle bridge or subway — 5 units.
Cost of cutting down trees — 10 units.
Cost of building a causeway over marshland — 20 units.
Cost of demolishing a house — 5 units.
Cost of buying land from the owner of Fyne Court — 20 units.

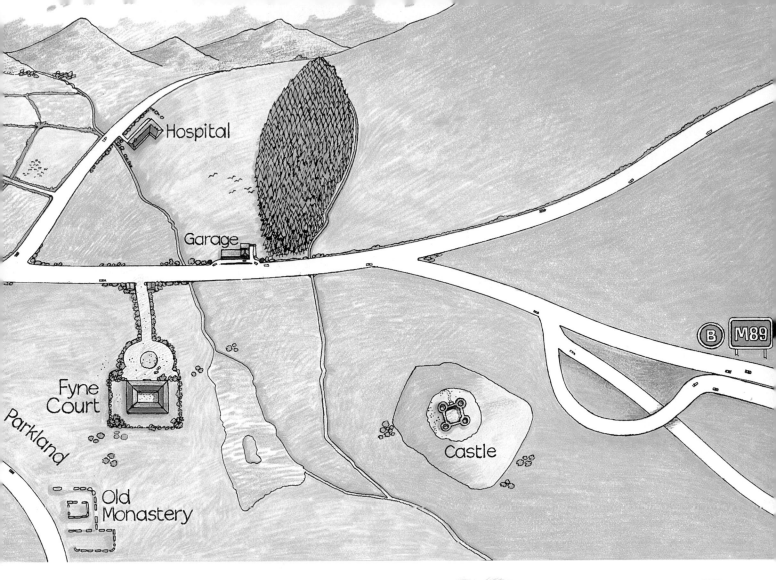

Part 2 The motorway inquiry

Here are some of the people from the area who attend the inquiry into the route you have chosen.

1. Write down what each person would say about your route and whether they would vote for it or not.
2. Write down the answer you would give to each person to tell them that your route is the best one. Remember to include in your answer details of the cost of building the motorway and how you have tried to avoid upsetting people.
3. Make a note of any changes you might make as a result of the arguments put forward at the inquiry.

We don't want the motorway near our houses.

Gerald Cuff
Residents Association

The old buildings must be protected. Don't spoil the castle approach.

Joan Entwistle
Preservation Society

Keep the motorway as straight as possible. Thank goodness there won't be any more traffic jams.

Jack Day
Lorry Owner

What's going to happen to all my passing trade?

Peter Harris
Garage Owner

The road will take trade away from the town. Keep away from the hospital.

Lucy Potter
Town Councillor

Keep orf my land. It will ruin the huntin!

Jeremy Cuthbert-Smith
Owner of Fyne Court

Checking

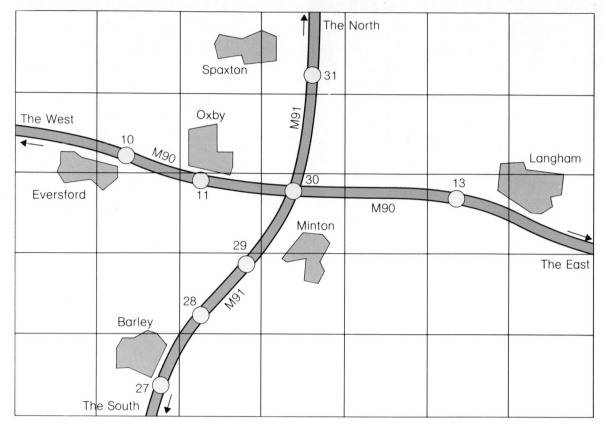

Thinking

1 What are the numbers of the motorway junctions where you would see the following five road signs?

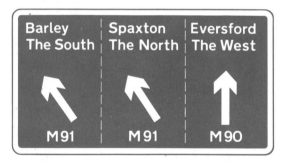

2 Look back at pages 72 and 73. If the Chards set off from Runcorn at 9.00 am on a Saturday morning, what time would they arrive in Clovelly?

Compare the two graphs showing the different parts of the journey. If there was a motorway between Taunton and Clovelly, how long would that part of the journey take?

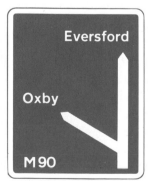

A class exercise

Choose a group of people in the class to act out the motorway inquiry on page 77. Two children could be motorway planners and show their different plans for the route. Each would try to prove that theirs was the best plan. Six children could act the parts of the people in the inquiry and put forward their arguments. One person could be the chairman to keep the meeting in order and to make sure everyone gets a chance to speak. At the end of the inquiry the rest of the class could vote for the best route.

Doing

In this picture are a number of signs and objects you are likely to see on a journey by road. What are they? The answers are at the foot of the page. Copy the signs on to a card and write what they are on the back. Make some more cards in the same way using different signs and objects. Now you can test your friends. You could also use them to play an eye-spy game on your next journey by road. Tick off each object on the card as you see it on the journey.

Going further

1   Use an atlas or road map to plan a journey from your home to a holiday town. Work out the distances and try to estimate how long the journey would take. On the motorway you could average 110 km.p.h. On an ordinary road you could average 55 km.p.h. Which towns would you pass through? Where would you stop for a meal? Draw a route diagram like David Chard's for your journey.

2   Many other countries have motorways. Each country has its own name for them. Match the motorway name to its country and write out the correct pairs.

Autobahn	USA
Autopista	Germany
Autostrada	France
Freeway	Italy
Autoroute	Spain

3   Ask a travel agent for holiday brochures for North Devon. Use the brochures and a map to plan the rest of the holiday week for the Chards.

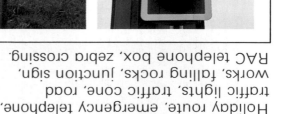

Holiday route, emergency telephone, traffic lights, traffic cone, road works, falling rocks, junction sign, RAC telephone box, zebra crossing.

Answers to signs

In the air

One weekend, Simon was helping his father dig the garden. As he walked across some newly dug soil he looked back at the footprints he had made. Here are the footprints.

They are plans of his feet.

Simon heard the sound of aeroplanes. He looked up in the sky and saw five aeroplanes flying in formation.

The pilot of the leading plane looked down. He could see Simon's garden below him. This is what he saw.

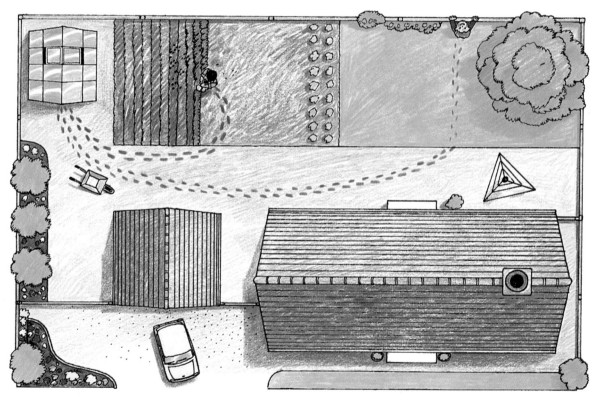

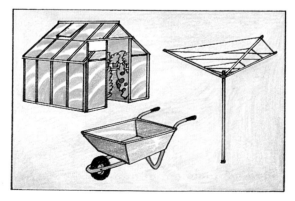

Find Simon's house, the vegetable patch and Simon's father.

Simon had left a trail of muddy footprints. Follow Simon's route. Use a piece of string to find out how far he has walked. How far is he now from each of the objects shown on the left? 1 centimetre on the plan represents 1 metre.

Simon stopped by the back fence. He looked up in the air and watched the planes. He noticed many other things happening in the sky. The picture above shows what he saw.

List the things which Simon could see.

Which way is the wind blowing? How can you tell? Name three things which are using the wind. Which entries in your list cause pollution? Remember that pollution can be caused by noise. Which objects are used for transporting man through the air?

Simon closed his eyes and listened carefully for two minutes. What are the noises Simon would be able to hear?

Next time you are outside, make a list of all the things you can see happening in the air. Close your eyes and find out how many sounds you can hear and identify.

Simon was especially interested in spotting aeroplanes because he was flying to Australia during the holidays to visit his relations. They had emigrated to Australia two years before. Simon was looking forward to seeing them again and making his first flight in an aeroplane. You can follow his journey on the following pages.

Spotting shapes

Notice how the aircraft have copied the flying formation of the geese. Each goose is flying in the slip-stream of the goose ahead. There is less air resistance this way so that energy is conserved. From time to time, another goose takes over the leading position.

81

At the airport

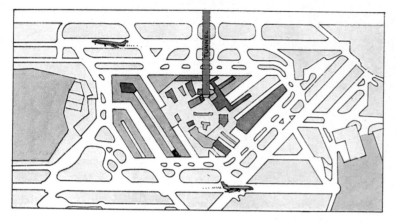

This is a plan of Heathrow airport near London. 15 million people pass through the airport every year. A plane takes off or lands every three minutes. Simon was travelling from Heathrow to Sydney in Australia.

Look at the plan of the airport. The runways surround the central arrival and departure area. There are two main runways. They run parallel on opposite sides of the airport. One runway is for taking off and one for landing. Wide concrete roads allow the planes to taxi from the central area to the runways. How did Simon get to the central area in safety?

Before Simon could board his plane he had to pass through different areas at the airport. The diagram below shows how arrivals and departures are routed through separate zones to keep the flow of people moving as efficiently as possible.

Follow Simon's route to his plane on the diagram.

1   **Check-in point** — Tickets are checked and boarding cards issued. Luggage is weighed and taken to the plane.
2   **Passport control** — Passports and hand luggage are checked.
3   **Departure lounge** — Passengers wait for their flights to be called. Refreshments are available and there are duty-free shops.
4   **Luggage collection point** — The luggage arrives on a conveyor belt from the plane.
5   **Customs** — Passengers follow the red channel if they are bringing goods into the country which have to be declared and an import duty paid on them. They follow the green channel if they have nothing to declare.

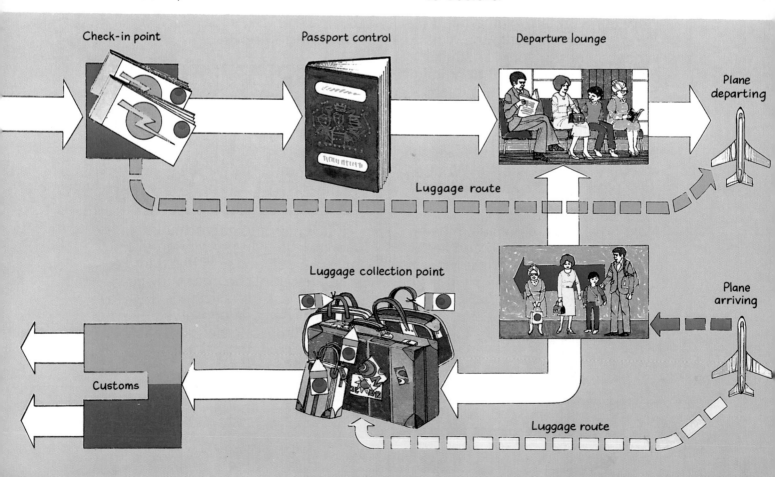

While Simon was waiting in the departure lounge for his flight to be called, he saw the supersonic airliner Concorde take off on a journey to America. Supersonic aircraft fly faster than the speed of sound. Concorde travels at 1600 km per hour and only takes $3\frac{1}{2}$ hours to reach New York.

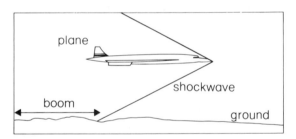

When Concorde, or any other supersonic aircraft, takes off the noise from its engines is very loud. When it exceeds the speed of sound it creates a shock wave which makes a loud noise or boom when it meets the ground. For this reason, the sites of airports have to be very carefully chosen and the flight paths planned so that as few people as possible are affected.

Sound levels round airports are carefully checked with sound meters. Subsidies are granted to house-holders near airports so that they can install double-glazing to their windows. Sound baffles are erected around the runways to absorb the noise. Airline pilots are asked to throttle back their engines as soon as possible after take-off.

Noise pollution from aircraft is a serious problem and new airports are being planned away from large centres of population. The plan below shows the area affected by high noise levels when Concorde takes off from Heathrow.

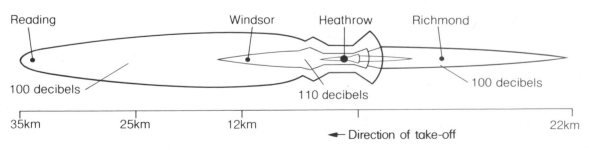

Travelling by air

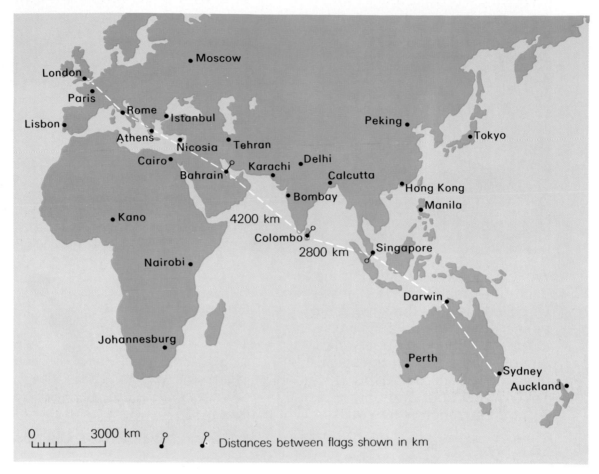

Moscow
London
Paris
Lisbon
Rome
Istanbul
Athens
Nicosia
Tehran
Cairo
Bahrain
Karachi
Delhi
Calcutta
Peking
Tokyo
Kano
Bombay
Hong Kong
Manila
4200 km
Colombo
2800 km
Singapore
Nairobi
Darwin
Johannesburg
Perth
Sydney
Auckland

0   3000 km   Distances between flags shown in km

This map shows the main airports in the eastern hemisphere where airliners call to pick up passengers or refuel. Simon's plane called at some of these airports.

The map shows the flight plan for Simon's journey. Copy out the flight plan and complete the flight distances.

Simon's plane can travel 6,000 km before it needs refuelling. If you were the flight controller, where would you arrange for refuelling to take place on the journey?

Plan a return journey for Simon from Sydney to London using a different route. Draw the flight plan you would use.

Plan a route from Tokyo to Johannesburg. At which airport could passengers from London join your flight?

Simon saw many aircraft at the airports where he stopped on his journey. He made a note of the airline emblems he saw on their tailplanes. Here are some of them. Write out the names of the airlines. Put the correct country next to each one, choosing from this list: Switzerland, Australia, Spain, USA, Japan, Holland, Ireland, Italy.

Aer Lingus   Pan Am   Alitalia

Qantas   Iberia

Swissair   KLM   JAL

84

On his journey, Simon flew over these places. Study your flight plan and the map at the top of page 84 and say where each place is.

Simon bought this postcard at his first stop on the journey.

Simon saw this scene from the porthole of the plane.

This is a photograph taken from space. It shows an area Simon flew over.

Below is a large-scale map of an area on Simon's route. Where is it? Name the islands.

Simon's plane flew high above the surface of the earth. There in the upper air the sky was clear. The plane flew above the clouds and avoided any bad weather below. On the last part of the journey the plane met strong headwinds as it flew across the sea area between Singapore and Darwin. The wind was blowing against the direction of the plane's flight and slowed down its movement through the air.

Simon looked out of the plane's porthole. All he could see below was a layer of cloud. The cloud stretched almost to the surface of the earth. At ground level, heavy rain was falling from the cloud. The next time the sky is overcast with cloud and it is raining hard, remember what it is like high up above the cloud.

By the time the plane reached Sydney the clouds had disappeared. Simon was very excited. He was looking forward to meeting his relations and to visiting one of the many fine beaches on the coast.

Checking

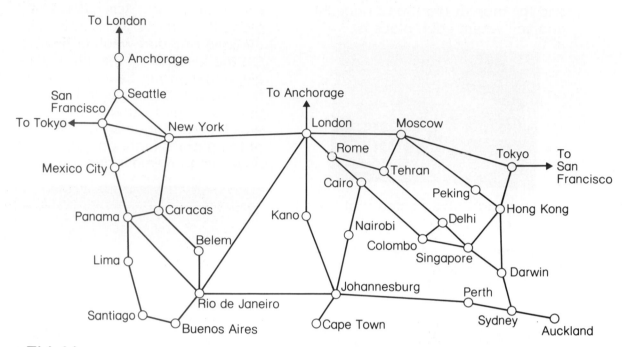

Thinking

1   This is a map of the major air routes in the world. It is a simplified map which does not show the outlines of the countries. Write down the routes for the following journeys: London to Auckland, London to Santiago, Tokyo to Sydney, Moscow to Mexico City, Sydney to Buenos Aires, Hong Kong to San Francisco, Rome to Anchorage.

The route from London to Anchorage passes over the polar region. As you can see from the diagram showing the earth as a globe, this is a much shorter distance than the route you would choose by looking at a flat map.

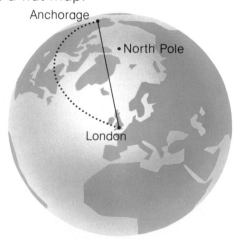

2   An airline is planning a route from New York to Sydney. It has also received bookings for the following journeys: Caracas to Rio de Janeiro, Buenos Aires to Johannesburg, Cape Town to Perth, Kano to Sydney.

The flight planner drew this flight plan. It shows the airports where the aircraft will land to pick up or put down passengers. It also shows the connecting flights which have been arranged to fit the bookings.

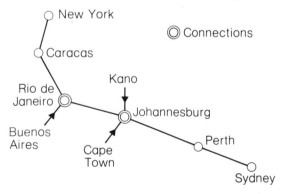

Draw a similar flight plan for a route from Santiago to Tokyo. You have received these additional bookings: Buenos Aires to Johannesburg, Panama to Delhi, Belem to Nairobi, Darwin to Tokyo, Colombo to Hong Kong.

Doing

Look at the diagrams and read the instructions to make your own supersonic paper aeroplane.

1 Fold over one corner of a rectangular piece of paper to make a square.
2 Cut off the piece left over to use as the tailplane. Make the folds as shown.
3 Push the centre folds inward to make a triangular shape. Press flat.
4 Fold **A** to the top point as shown. Do the same with **B**.
5 Fold along the dotted line on both sides of the centre as shown.
6 Fold over points **A** and **B** into the pockets.
7 Fold corners **C** and **D** on the tailplane.
8 Insert tail section and fold back point of aeroplane.
9 Now your plane is ready to fly. Decorate it with an airline emblem and launch it, holding it below the wings.

Going further

Look at the map showing a large city and its airport. The amount of air transport has grown too great for the one airport to handle. Three places have been suggested as possible sites for a new airport.

List the advantages and disadvantages of each possible site. Where would you build the new airport? Give reasons for your choice. Would your choice require changes to be made, such as the building of a new road?

Copy the map, show the site of your new airport and any changes you would make.

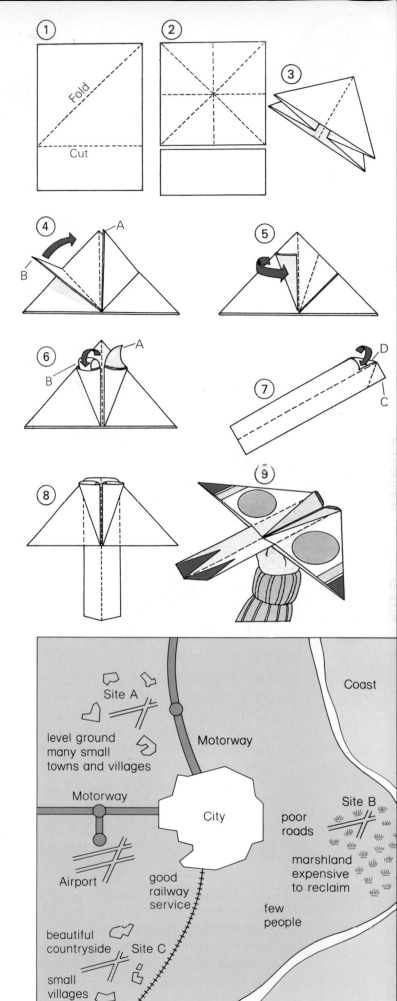

87

Hills and valleys

This is the valley of the River Wint. Look closely at the picture. Find the castle, the two villages, the quarry and the prehistoric settlement on the hilltop. Trace the course of the river and count the number of streams which join it. Where do the streams come from?

On the far side of the valley you can see three farms. The farmhouses have been built close to springs flowing out of the hillside. The tops of the hills are covered in short, rough grass. The wide valley has fields of lush meadowland bordering the river. What kind of animals are kept (a) on the hills; (b) in the valley?

There are three types of settlement shown on the picture: a prehistoric settlement, a castle and villages.

Describe where each type of settlement is found and why. Here are some clues about each place.

1   The top of the hill is easy to defend.
2   Invading armies would come through the gap in the ridge of hills.
3   The bottom of the valley is sheltered from the wind. It has better farming land.

Match the correct settlement to each clue.

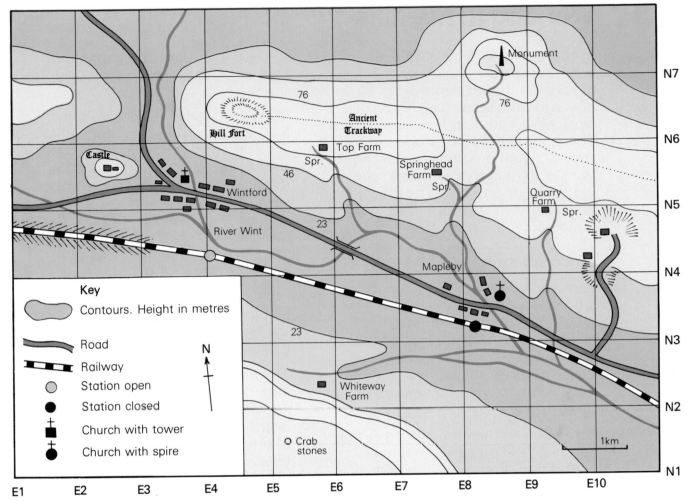

Key

	Contours. Height in metres
	Road
	Railway
○	Station open
●	Station closed
✠	Church with tower
✝	Church with spire

N

The Wint valley

This is a map of the Wint valley. The picture on page 88 was drawn from the point marked crab stones (E5N1). Look carefully at both the picture and the map and answer these ten quick questions.

1 Give the square reference for the castle.
2 Give the square reference for the quarry.
3 Give the square reference for the church at Mapleby.
4 What is the meaning of Spr. at E5N5, E7N5 and E9N4?
5 At which village can you still catch a train?
6 What is there in square E4N6?
7 What is there in square E3N5?
8 What is there in square E8N7?
9 Why can't you see Whiteway Farm (E5N2) in the picture?
10 How far is it from Wintford to Mapleby?

The road and railway run along the valley at the bottom of the hills to avoid any steep gradients. Think what might happen if there was very heavy rain on the hills. The streams would fill with water and cascade down the hillside into the river. Eventually the river might overflow its banks and the whole valley would be flooded.

The railway is raised above the floor of the valley on an embankment. Look how the embankment is shown on the map.

In prehistoric times the valley would be very marshy and full of thick woodland. The best place to travel would be along the tops of the hills. Find the ancient track leading to the hill fort.

Working in the hills

In the quarry large blocks of stone are blasted from the rock face. The blocks are then cut into slabs by powerful machine saws. The noise is deafening and dust flies everywhere. The slabs are polished and cut to shape. Some are used for building houses, others for fireplaces, garden walls or gravestones. The chippings which are left over are used for road building.

The crab stones

Did you wonder what the crab stones were used for? They are the remains of an earlier type of quarrying. Look back at the picture on page 88. You can just see the quarry hole by the stones. It is now nearly covered by brambles.

This is what it used to look like. Can you see the crab stones in the centre of the picture? They are supporting a revolving capstan or spindle. The quarry hole is at the back of the picture on the left-hand side.

A wooden beam has been placed across the entrance to the hole for safety.

Blocks of stone were hewn out from underground and dragged to the bottom of the hole. They were fastened to a chain and pulled up the slope by a horse who walked round the spindle winding in the chain. Young boys helped the men at the bottom of the hole. Sometimes the spindle was turned by girls instead of by a horse.

From the picture on page 88 you can tell that the quarry is in the hills. Would you know this from looking at the map?

The map shows you the shape of the land by using contour lines. Find the black contour lines on the map of the Wint valley. They join places of the same height. The lines tell you where the hills and valleys are, where there is high and low land and steep slopes. On some of the lines the height of the land above sea-level is marked.

Class 4 made a model to help them find out more about contour lines.

First of all they made a plasticine island and moulded it so that it had hills and a valley.

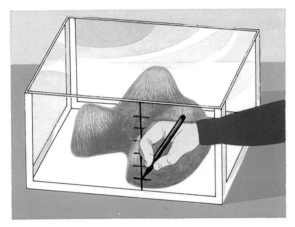

Then they put the island into an empty fish tank. Gordon marked a scale down the side of the tank.

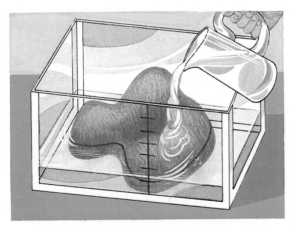

Joanna poured water into the tank until the water level reached the first mark on the scale. Peter used a waterproof marker to mark the line the water had reached on the model.

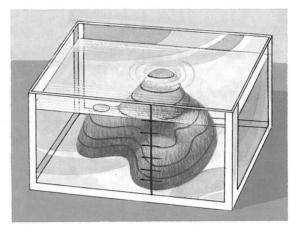

They did this several times, pouring in more water and marking the different water levels on the model.

Then they carefully lifted the model out of the tank. The lines they had marked were contour lines.

Susan looked at the model from above and made this sketch showing the shape of the island and the contour lines. She marked the valley. Notice how the shape of the contour lines show where the valley is. How can you tell which is the steepest slope?

The story of a river

Source

High in the hills water runs down the slopes and collects in streams. These form the source (**A**) or start of the river on its long journey to the sea. The slopes are steep and the water runs swiftly. The current of the stream is strong enough to move stones and pebbles which cut into the stream bed, making both the river and the valley deeper.

Waterfall and gorge

More streams join the main river. These streams are called tributaries (**B**). Where the river reaches a sudden break in the hill slope, it cascades over a waterfall (**C**) into a large, deep pool below. The increased force of the water gradually wears away the rock so that the waterfall moves further and further upstream. You can see in the picture how far the river has worn back the waterfall from the original break in the hill slope. The deep narrow valley which it has made here is called a gorge (**D**).

Lower valley

Gradually the land becomes flatter and the river flows more slowly. It is wider and begins to wind in great loops across its valley. The loops are called meanders (**E**).

The valley is very wide and flat now. This is the area which will flood if there are heavy rainstorms in the hills and the river level rises with the increased amount of water.

Estuary

Finally the river reaches the sea. The wide mouth of the river is called an estuary (**F**). It is wide and deep enough for large ships to sail into the port on its bank.

Here are some words to describe the movement of a river: gurgle, swirl, plunge, wind, race, eddy. Think of more words to add to the list. Use them to write your own poem about a river.

Checking

Thinking

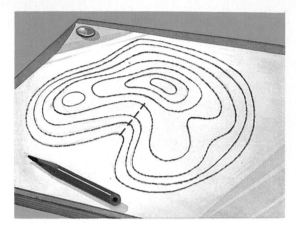

1 This is a map of the model shown on page 91. What are the lines on the map called? What do they tell you about the shape of the hill and its slopes?

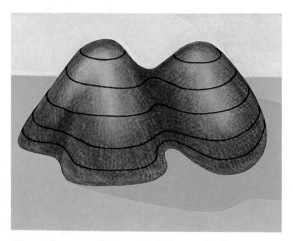

Here is another model made by class 4 and marked in the same way as the one on page 91. Draw a map of the model.

2 Copy out the sentences below and insert the correct word in each gap.

The start of a river is called its _____. _____ are streams and rivers which join a main river. A deep, narrow valley is called a _____. The river winds across the valley in loops or _____. This part of the river could easily _____ if there was a heavy rainstorm upstream. The river widens to form an _____ where it meets the sea.

3 These pictures show four different stages in a river's course. Look back at pages 92 and 93. Decide what each picture shows. Label each one and put the correct letter by its name.

Talking

Look at the picture of the Wint valley on page 88. Describe a walk through the valley, giving as much detail as possible. See if your friend can trace your path on the map.

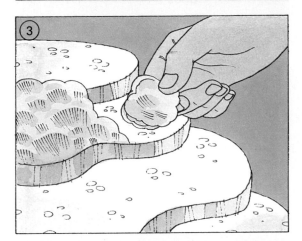

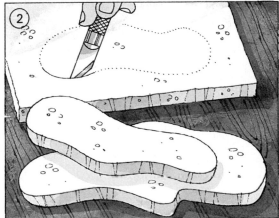

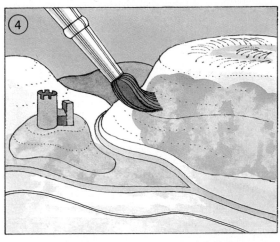

Going further

Use the map on page 89 to help you make a detailed model of the Wint valley.

1   Copy the map on to a piece of paper, making it twice as big. Stick the paper on to a board.

2   Trace the outlines of the contours and cut out each shape from a piece of polystyrene (ceiling tiles would be suitable). When you have cut out all the shapes, glue them together in the correct order and stick them on to the map.

3   Fill in the steps with plasticine, papier maché or plaster to give the hills a smooth surface.

4   Now you can paint the model and add houses, rivers, roads, railways, the castle and any other features. Does your model look like the picture on page 88?

Puzzle picture – the river which turned into a stone wall. Where did the river go? The diagram will help.

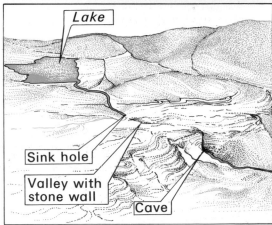

Lake

Sink hole

Valley with stone wall

Cave

Synopsis

Oxford New Geography is a complete four-book course for juniors. It introduces the basic skills and concepts of the New Geography at the primary level. The four books are each divided into three sections.

Explorations

How do I find out? How do I record? These and other basic questions are used to develop skills needed by children for a purposeful exploration of the environment. By the use of actual situations children are shown how to look around classroom, school, houses, streets, parks, etc. Familiar situations are used as a springboard for the exploration of less familiar and distant environments.

Face to Face

The emphasis is on presenting lively accounts of people in key occupations as a means of studying the world of work and leisure. Case studies of farms, factories, life in cities and the countryside are used. Children are encouraged to draw comparisons and contrasts with the world they know both at home and abroad.

Links

How are things related and interdependent? From the story of how we get our daily milk and mail to the world of commuters and motorways, the series traces the links that make modern life possible.

The sections contain an average of four units. The units are organized in double-page spreads enabling full use to be made of colour illustrations. The last spread in each unit is used for checking over the work and suggesting lines of further development. Exercises, games and activities cover a wide range of basic geographical skills and concepts.

The Publisher would like to thank the following for permission to reproduce photographs:

Aero & Industrial Photographic Services, p 59; Aerofilms, p 3 (top left & right); Aspect Bob Davis, pp 41, 85 (bottom right); Mike Baker, p 15 (bottom left); Barnaby's Picture Library, pp 9, 20 (centre left); 32 (top centre), 66, 67 (top left); BBC TV/Michael Fish, Meteorological Office, pp 30, 33; Steve Benbow, p 20 (bottom left); British Airways, p 83 (top); Brockhole, p 21; Camera Press/The Observer, p 83 (right); Bruce Coleman, pp 20 (top left), 25 (bottom left & right); Colorsport, p 54; Ian Condon, p 15 (top right); Crown Copyright, pp 31, 32 (bottom); Daily Telegraph Colour Library, pp 41 (3), 69; Departments of the Environment & Transport, pp 75, 79; Devon News Service, p 28; J. Arthur Dixon, p 2; Dorset County Museum, pp 10, 12, 90; Educational Productions Ltd, p 95; Electricity Council, p 71; Fifa/Syndication International, p 55; Susan Griggs, p 85 (top left); J. E. L. Hulbert, p 32 (bottom centre); Institution of Civil Engineers, pp 28/29; Manhattan Post Card Co Inc, p 2; Bob Matthews, p 21; John Mills/Runcorn Development Corp, p 45 (top left); Nobu Miyazaki, p 67; Colin Molyneux, p 20 (top & bottom right, centre); NASA, p 85 (top left); Nottingham Forest Football Club, p 50; North American Soccer League, pp 56/57; Nu-colorvue Productions Pty Ltd, p 2; PAAT, Oxford, pp 9 (top right), 17, 32, 72; T. I. Raleigh Ltd, p 67 (right); Simon Stafford, pp 11, 13, 14, 15, 38 (right), 79; John Sims, p 62 (left); Space Frontiers, p 85 (top right); Spectrum, p 62 (right); Syndication International, pp 50 (bottom), 53; Jeffrey Tabberner, pp 34, 36 (top & bottom), 37 (top & bottom), 38 (left), 39 (left & right); Topix, p 29; Truckline Ferries Poole Ltd. pp 60/61; Vision International, p 18, 25 (top left); West Air Photography, p 35; Brian Williams/Runcorn Development Corporation, pp 42, 43, 45, 47; J. R. Wooldridge, p 20 (centre right).

Book 1

Explorations
Unit 1   Warm and dry
Unit 2   Playspace
Unit 3   Look around

Face to Face
Unit 4   Ash Farm
Unit 5   The fire
Unit 6   Hill View Farm

Links
Unit 7   Links
Unit 8   Milk break
Unit 9   In the forest

Book 2

Explorations
Unit 1   The street
Unit 2   Then and now
Unit 3   Shops
Unit 4   Weather

Face to Face
Unit 5   An English steelworker
Unit 6   A Brazilian steelworker
Unit 7   The docks
Unit 8   A dustman

Links
Unit 9   To and from the docks
Unit 10   Coal
Unit 11   Mountains
Unit 12   Water

Book 3

Explorations
Unit 1   The neighbourhood
Unit 2   A neighbourhood then and now
Unit 3   Pollution
Unit 4   Harness the wind

Face to Face
Unit 5   Making cars
Unit 6   A Japanese car worker
Unit 7   Farming
Unit 8   Rich and poor

Links
Unit 9   Links in the countryside
Unit 10   Links in action
Unit 11   Growing food
Unit 12   Rocks

Illustrated by John Hunt, Ben Manchipp, Edward McLachlan, Miller, Craig & Cocking, Barry Rowe, Simon Stafford, Michael Whittlesea. Cover illustration by Ronald Maddox.

Picture Research by Ann Usborne
Design by Stafford & Stafford, Oxford

© Keith Martin 1980

First published 1980
Reprinted 1981, 1982, 1987

Oxford University Press, Walton Street, Oxford OX2 6DP

Oxford New York Toronto
Delhi Bombay Calcutta Madras Karachi
Petaling Jaya Singapore Hong Kong Tokyo
Nairobi Dar es Salaam Cape Town
Melbourne Auckland

and associated companies in
Beirut Berlin Ibadan Nicosia

Oxford is a trade mark of Oxford University Press

Filmset by Tradespools Ltd, Frome, Somerset
Printed in Hong Kong

ISBN 0 19 917026 6